As someone who regularly lac[
God is doing good things, even
Waiting with Hope offers potent, grace-filled encouragement for
weary, impatient hearts like mine. This book will encourage you to
look to our perfect example of patience, Christ Jesus, and remember his tender faithfulness not only to you but to all his people. I
can't recommend it highly enough!

    —**Hunter Beless**, Founder and Host, *Journeywomen* podcast

This devotional was exactly what I needed to read during a season of wearying hardship. As Megan skillfully guides readers into
the riches of God's Word, she strikes the kind of careful balance
between comfort and counsel that refreshes our hearts while
maturing us in Christ at the very same time. If you're looking to
grow in patience, don't wait to get this book.

    —**Christine Chappell**, Outreach Director, Institute for Bibli-
      cal Counseling & Discipleship; Host, *Hope + Help Podcast*

Christians often joke about being careful not to pray for patience
because God will give us the opportunity to learn it. In *Patience:
Waiting with Hope*, readers will see that growth in patience is in fact
a good thing. As Megan Hill reveals, it is good to wait on the Lord,
for he does good things within us while we wait—cultivating the
fruit of patience in our hearts. Instead of avoiding these important
lessons, may we yield to the Spirit's work and desire to grow in our
patience with God, our circumstances, and one another.

    —**Christina Fox**, Counselor; Speaker; Author, *A Holy Fear:
      Trading Lesser Fears for the Fear of the Lord*

Patience proves to be one of the rarest of virtues. Yet it is one of
the attributes that marks our holy God and, therefore, is to mark
his holy people. Every Christian could use a little more reflection
and encouragement to grow in this fruit of the Spirit. Megan Hill
has blessed the church in providing a devotional for this very purpose. These helpful daily readings will serve those who are serious

about their faith and long to look more like their God—who is "slow to anger and abounding in steadfast love." Read, meditate, pray, and grow in the virtue of patience.

—**Jason Helopoulos**, Senior Pastor, University Reformed Church, East Lansing, Michigan; Author; Series Editor, The Blessings of the Faith

Patience is not something that can be acquired overnight. It is the fruit of many small choices, day by day, to trust God's timing rather than our own. These short daily readings from Megan Hill are an ideal way to cultivate the fruit of patience. Hill takes Bible passages on patience and helps the reader to apply them in ways that are both realistic and life-giving. Read one each morning, and look for an opportunity to put it into practice!

—**Betsy Childs Howard**, Editor, The Gospel Coalition; Author, *Seasons of Waiting: Walking by Faith When Dreams Are Delayed*

This excellent book not only teaches us the truth about godly patience but is structured to help us to develop what it promotes. In devotions that take just a few minutes to read each day, Megan Hill offers anxious souls the spiritual training necessary to build the muscles of godly patience. Having defined patience biblically, she points us to the character of God, she brings us to Christ, and she helps us to practice patience amid daily trials and in light of eternal realities. This is a much-needed help to weary souls in anxious times!

—**David Strain**, Senior Pastor, First Presbyterian Church, Jackson, Mississippi

Patience may be the most misunderstood and undervalued fruit of the Spirit. Therefore, I am grateful for this insightful devotional—and to Megan Hill for skillfully employing God's Word to help us to see the myriad ways impatience shows up in our hearts. Most importantly, while rooting the virtue of patience in the long-suffering of God and fueling our sanctification with gospel hope, the author helps us to see what putting on Christlike patience looks like in the practical ins and outs of daily life. This devotional gently unleashes the life-changing power of Scripture.

—**Paul Tautges**, Author, *Anxiety: Knowing God's Peace*; Senior Pastor, Cornerstone Community Church, Mayfield Heights, Ohio; Founder, Counseling One Another

PATIENCE

31-Day Devotionals for Life

A Series

Deepak Reju
Series Editor

PATIENCE

WAITING WITH HOPE

MEGAN HILL

PUBLISHING
P.O. BOX 817 • PHILLIPSBURG • NEW JERSEY 08865-0817

Unless otherwise indicated, Scripture quotations are from the ESV Bible® (The Holy Bible, English Standard Version®), copyright © 2001 by Crossway, a publishing ministry of Good News Publishers. Used by permission. All rights reserved.

Scripture quotations marked (NIV) are taken from the Holy Bible, New International Version®, NIV®. Copyright © 1973, 1978, 1984, 2011 by Biblica, Inc.™ Used by permission of Zondervan. All rights reserved worldwide. www.zondervan.com. The "NIV" and "New International Version" are trademarks registered in the United States Patent and Trademark Office by Biblica, Inc.™

Scripture quotations from the New Testament use the ESV's alternate, footnoted translation of *adelphoi* ("brothers and sisters").

Italics within Scripture quotations indicate emphasis added.

Printed in the United States of America

Library of Congress Cataloging-in-Publication Data

Names: Hill, Megan, author.
Title: Patience : waiting with hope / Megan Hill.
Description: Phillipsburg, New Jersey : P&R Publishing, [2021] | Series: 31-day devotionals for life | Includes bibliographical references. | Summary: "We often confuse patience with bitter endurance. It's not! Megan Hill shows us what-and Who-biblical patience looks like and how to make it a part of daily life"-- Provided by publisher.
Identifiers: LCCN 2021019576 | ISBN 9781629958118 (paperback) | ISBN 9781629958125 (epub) | ISBN 9781629958132 (mobi)
Subjects: LCSH: Patience--Religious aspects--Christianity. | Patience--Biblical teaching. | Devotional literature.
Classification: LCC BV4647.P3 H55 2021 | DDC 241/.4--dc23
LC record available at https://lccn.loc.gov/2021019576

Contents

How to Nourish Your Soul

A LITTLE BIT *every day* can do great good for your soul.

I read the Bible to my kids during breakfast. I don't read a lot. Maybe just a few verses. But I work hard to do it every weekday.

My wife and I pray for one of our children, a different child each night, before we go to bed. We usually take just a few minutes. We don't pray lengthy, expansive prayers. But we try to do this most every night.

Although they don't take long, these practices are edifying, hopeful, and effective.

This devotional is just the same. Each entry is short. Just a few tasty morsels of Scripture to nourish your hungry soul. Read it on the subway or the bus on the way to work. Read it with a friend or a spouse every night at dinner. Make it a part of each day for thirty-one days, and it will do you great good.

Why is that?

We start with Scripture. God's Word is powerful. Used by the Holy Spirit, it turns the hearts of kings, brings comfort to the lowly, and gives spiritual sight to the blind. It transforms lives and turns them upside down. We know that the Bible is God's very own words, so we read and study it to know God himself.

Our study of Scripture is practical. Theology should change how we live. It's crucial to connect the Word with your struggles. Often, as you read this devotional, you'll see the word *you* because Megan speaks directly to you, the reader. Each reading contains reflection questions and a practical suggestion. You'll get much more from this experience if you answer the questions and do the practical exercises. Don't skip them. Do them for the sake of your own soul.

Our study of Scripture is worshipful. Maybe your experiences this past week included something like this: You got frustrated because you were stuck in a long line or in another traffic jam. You rushed through your daily Bible reading. You got annoyed as you were interrupted while working on a project. You felt frustrated as a friend or your child complained (yet again). If you look around your life, you'll find signs of impatience everywhere. That's why God's Word matters. Your sin makes you an impatient person. You can't grow in patience on your own. You need a Savior who is merciful, long-suffering, and patient with you and who, in turn, leads you to be grateful for him. What should your study of the Word lead you to? Worship of him. Every time you run into your impatience, it should be a reminder: "I can't do this on my own; I need Jesus to help me." You need a Savior who can rescue you from your sin and give you the gift of patience, not just one time but daily. As you study your Bible, you will learn that God has a lot to say about patience, and he will help you to grow in it.

If you find this devotional helpful (and I trust that you will!), reread it in different seasons of your life. It will help to remind you of God's goodness and power and promises whenever you have to be patient. So work through it this coming month and then come back to it a year from now to remind yourself about what God and his gospel teach us about cultivating patience.

This devotional starts you on a wonderful journey of growing in patience. After you finish reading (and rereading) it, if you want more, you'll see additional resources listed at the end of the book. Buy them and make good use of them.

Are you ready? Let's begin.

Deepak Reju

Introduction

WE LIVE IN an impatient world. All around us, people are constantly seeking a fast track to fulfilled desire. Our friends and neighbors want what they want, and they want it yesterday. For Christians, too, the temptation to impatience is powerful. We know we should be patient, but we are tired of waiting.

Sometimes, we are tired of waiting on God to grant healing, to give financial stability, to bless us with children or a spouse, to prosper our work, or to lessen our afflictions. We long for the day when our loved ones come to faith or our church begins to grow, but God seems to be delaying. We don't know how long we can continue to live in hope.

Other times, we are tired of bearing with others: the annoying church member, the immature child, the imperfect spouse, the needy friend, or the hostile coworker. No matter how often we repeat ourselves or speak kindly to them, these people seem intent on frustrating us. We may be ashamed to admit it, but we secretly wish we didn't have to constantly interact with them. In other cases, we want the people we love to change for their own good—to conquer their addictions, to develop productive habits, or to know Christ more—but the transformation seems to be happening excruciatingly slowly, if at all. We'd like to be hopeful, but as time passes, we feel like giving up.

Impatience is bad enough on its own, but once it seizes our hearts, it quickly produces additional sins. Looking for a way to get what we want *now*, we run headlong down disobedient paths. Like King Saul, who got tired of waiting for God's priest and rashly offered the sacrifice himself (see 1 Sam. 13:8–15), we grasp at any means to end the wait. We accumulate credit card debt, marry unbelievers, accept unethical business practices, fall into sexual sin, compromise the gospel message, and manipulate others in order to fulfill our desires on our own schedule. We seethe with envy when friends and neighbors receive the very thing we've been waiting for, and we lash out in anger toward anything and anyone who stands in our way. Our honking horns and harsh words are symptoms of our daily unwillingness to wait a moment longer than we deem necessary. More quietly, but no less destructively, our impatience also creates anxiety in our hearts. When God appears slow to act, we worry that he never will. Our doubts about God's trustworthiness begin to shake our faith. We focus on our own timetable and fret with every seemingly unproductive day that passes.

This impatience harms others. The people in our homes and workplaces instinctively start to approach us with fear—not knowing when we might explode in their direction. They notice our lack of trust in God's sovereign timing and begin to eye their own calendars and circumstances with worry. Perhaps, they think, God isn't who he says he is after all. Our friends and neighbors also witness our immoral shortcuts and consider whether they might be justified in doing the same. Like the people of Israel who led each other into disaster, impatiently presuming to enter the land when God had told them to wait (see Num. 14:39–45), we can easily cause those around us to sin.

Thankfully, God's redeemed people don't need to be captive to impatience. Because of Christ's perfect obedience, his death on the cross, and his resurrection and ascension, we are no longer slaves to our sin (see Rom. 6:17–18). And because his Spirit lives in us, he cultivates the spiritual fruit of patience in our lives (see Gal. 5:22). What's more, we serve a God who is himself long-suffering—when we confess our impatience, we find that he is full of grace for short-tempered people (see Ex. 34:6).

Over the next thirty-one days, we'll be studying how to grow in patience. Simply put, patience is faithfulness over time. It's the diligent practice of godliness while you wait—whether you're waiting on people, on circumstances, or, ultimately, on God. It's waiting well. It's waiting with hope.

On each day this month, we will meditate on what the Bible says about the blessing of patience and the danger of impatience. Only the Word of God, accompanied by the work of his Spirit, can inform our consciences and compel our actions. For this reason, it's important to prayerfully read the Scripture verses at the beginning of each devotional and also to look up other referenced texts. It may be tempting to skip and skim. Don't. The Lord changes our hearts as we meditate on his Word.

Beginning with a biblical vision for waiting well, we'll examine various aspects of patience (days 1–4) and answer the question *What, exactly, is patience?* Then we'll consider why we should wait (days 5–9), unpacking biblical incentives for patience. Next we'll look to Christ to teach us about patience (days 10–13). We cannot presume to understand patience apart from Christ or to practice it without his help. We'll continue by seeking to develop a right understanding of time and our circumstances (days 14–20) and establish godly priorities for what we should do while we wait (days 21–25). Although we may often think of patience as passive, we'll discover that it actually requires diligent activity. Finally, we'll learn to pursue Christlike patience in several circumstances that commonly tempt us to impatience (days 26–30) and conclude with a look at how our own experience of waiting can help other impatient people (day 31). Through his Word and his Spirit, we'll see that God has given us everything we need to wait with hope.

You may want to use this devotional on your own as part of your daily prayer and Bible reading. Or perhaps you'll use it under the direction of your pastor or another counselor as part of a plan to fight the sin of impatience in your life. You may also want to use this book with a friend or a small group, encouraging one another and holding one another accountable for waiting well in all the large and small trials of life.

For impatient people, thirty-one days to cultivate patience may seem like a long time. In truth, it will probably take a lifetime. But out of obedience to the Lord, we "put on then, as God's chosen ones, holy and beloved, compassionate hearts, kindness, humility, meekness, and patience" (Col. 3:12). We rely on his Spirit, trust his grace, meditate on his Word, seek his forgiveness, and "put on . . . patience"—day after day after day, hoping for that glorious day when we will be made like our perfectly patient Savior forever.

UNDERSTANDING
PATIENCE

Over the next few days, we'll look at how the Bible defines patience, as it relates to both our circumstances and our relationships. Having a clear, constructive understanding of patience will equip us to cultivate it in our lives.

Patience Is Waiting on the Lord

*I waited patiently for the LORD; he inclined to
me and heard my cry. (Ps. 40:1)*

WHAT IS PATIENCE? It may be a familiar word, but I suspect we're more likely to define it by what it's *not* than what it *is*. Patience, we think, is not pacing the room while I wait for that important phone call. It's not fussing at my dawdling teenager or honking at the elderly driver in front of me. Patience is not grumbling, fretting, or exploding when I experience a delay. But the Bible also presents patience as a positive virtue. It's not merely the absence of sin; it's the pursuit of righteousness. Today we'll see that patience is waiting on the Lord. The Lord is sovereign over the circumstances and people in our lives; ultimately, he is the one who causes us to wait, and he brings our waiting to an end. We practice patience by looking in faith to him.

In Psalm 40, David is stuck. He's trapped in a "pit of destruction" and floundering in a "miry bog" (v. 2). The psalm doesn't explain exactly what David's swamp was; it could have been a work struggle or a relational mess. It could have been both. But, whatever the circumstances, David's response was to cry out to God and then wait. And because he studied God's Word and works (vv. 5, 7–8), meditated on God's kindness and mercy (vv. 6, 11), and diligently participated in corporate worship (vv. 9–10), David waited with hope. We can learn from his example. Whether we are stuck in unmet desires or tangled in financial worries, we can call on our Lord. We can seek to know him as he is revealed in his Word. And we can trust he will do what is best.

In the end, God always keeps perfect time.[1] He never underestimates the amount of time it will take to accomplish a goal or to bring about a certain result. He never misjudges his own ability; he never miscalculates the moment to act. Because he is sovereign over all, his plans and purposes unfold precisely when they should, at the very moment he decreed from eternity past. Every one of God's works happens exactly on time.

This is why David could say in another psalm, "Wait for the LORD; be strong, and let your heart take courage; wait for the LORD!" (27:14). Our souls should be encouraged when we realize it's God we're waiting on. Unlike fallible people, God has never had to rush in and say to anyone, "I'm so sorry I kept you waiting." If the Lord delays, it's not because he miscalculated. We can wait with hope, knowing he has wisely determined that this precise period of waiting is the best thing for our good and his glory.

Let your heart take courage.

Reflect: How do you typically define patience? What do you think it's *not*? What do you think it *is*?

Reflect: Read Psalm 27. What are some of the difficult situations David describes? Can you relate? What does David say he is seeking in the midst of trouble? How does seeking God reorient your perspective while you wait on him?

Act: No matter what you are waiting on today, you are ultimately waiting on the Lord. Cry out to him, seek him in the Scriptures, and ask for the Spirit's help to trust that he will act at just the right time.

DAY 2

Patience Is Steadfastness

You also, be patient. Establish your hearts, for the coming of the
Lord is at hand. . . . As an example of suffering and patience, brothers
and sisters, take the prophets who spoke in the name of the Lord. Behold,
we consider those blessed who remained steadfast. (James 5:8, 10–11)

IN 1858, John G. Paton and his wife arrived on the South Sea island of Tanna, hoping to bring the good news of Christ to the island's yet-unreached population. A few months later, Paton's wife and infant son died, leaving him alone among a hostile, cannibalistic people. As he labored, Paton suffered debilitating illnesses, mistreatment, robbery, and repeated threats to his life. He nevertheless traveled the island, preaching the gospel and constantly praying for the Lord to work savingly in Tanna. After three years, he had to flee to Australia for his life. He had witnessed only a few conversions.[1]

Patience is rarely glamorous. In biblical terms, patience often means "steadfastness" and "endurance." It's a virtue for Christians stuck in dead-end jobs, living with chronic illness, plagued with spiritual doubts, or beset by sin. When today feels like a discouraging repeat of yesterday, you need patience.

Writing to churches experiencing hardship, James exhorts believers to be patient, to establish their hearts, and to remain steadfast. Steadfastness is faithfulness in difficult circumstances. In other parts of his epistle, James explores ways that such steadfastness is essential to the life of faith: The steadfast person is better able to act wisely (1:5–8), to withstand temptation to sin (1:12–15), and to practice righteousness (1:19–25). Like the Old Testament prophets, the steadfast person can proclaim Christ in the face of opposition and while seeing little fruit (5:10). Like Job,

17

the steadfast person can trust God in the midst of physical suffering (5:11). Like Elijah, the steadfast person can keep praying even when he or she feels weak (5:17–18). And practicing steadfastness produces further steadfastness (1:2–4). James's teaching affirms that patience is not an optional discipline. To glorify God in a fallen world, Christians *need* patience (see Heb. 10:36).

Having called us to patience, James encourages us in our calling by lifting our eyes to the future: "The coming of the Lord is at hand." Even a hostile work environment or yearslong struggle with spiritual depression has an expiration date. One day—a day that is so close James says it's "at hand"—the Lord will return and our faithfulness will not have been in vain.

For the rest of his life, John G. Paton continued to pray for the Tannese people and asked the church to pray for them too. Thirty-four years after he left the island, the Lord raised up a new missionary. Under the preaching of Paton's son Frank, the Tannese people finally embraced Christ. The prayers of one generation were answered in the next, and, in eternity, father and son will both be commended for their steadfast endurance.

Reflect: "You have need of endurance," writes the author of Hebrews (10:36). Do you think of yourself as needing endurance? When you understand that patience is essential, how does that influence your desire to cultivate it in your own life?

Reflect: Read Job 1. How were Job's trials an opportunity for him to practice steadfastness?

Act: A circumstance we can easily bear for a single day will often seem overwhelming if we think about having to bear it for the next twenty years. Heed the words of Jesus: "Do not be anxious about tomorrow, for tomorrow will be anxious for itself. Sufficient for the day is its own trouble" (Matt. 6:34). Don't focus on tomorrow. Seek the Spirit's help to remain steadfast today.

DAY 3

Patience Is Long-Suffering

*I . . . urge you to walk in a manner worthy of the calling to
which you have been called, with all humility and gentleness, with
patience, bearing with one another in love, eager to maintain
the unity of the Spirit in the bond of peace. (Eph. 4:1–3)*

WHEN WAS THE last time someone sinned against you? It
probably wasn't long ago. In hundreds of ways, even among other
Christians, we experience mistreatment. Peter, too, knew first-
hand about being repeatedly slighted and elbowed by his fellow
disciples, and so he asked Jesus whether there was a limit to what
he could be expected to endure: "Lord, how often will my brother
sin against me, and I forgive him? As many as seven times?"
(Matt. 18:21). In reply, Christ commands patience beyond
anything Peter imagined: "I do not say to you seven times, but
seventy-seven times" (v. 22).

As we define patience, we see today that patience is long-
suffering with people who sin against us. In today's verses, Paul
exhorts the members of the church at Ephesus to "walk . . . with
patience, bearing with one another in love." Paul and Jesus shared
the same realistic view of the Christian life: Being sinned against
is inevitable. We can count on being sinned against many, many
times. We ought not to be caught off guard when someone speaks
untruthfully of us, when someone cuts us off midsentence in
order to focus on themselves, or when someone fails to see our
need for help and prayer. Because we live in a fallen world among
sinful people, we will regularly get hurt.

The surprise is not that we are sinned against. The surprise
is the patient way that God's people react to their injuries. The
people of this world are quick to seek personal retribution for

the smallest insult. Like Lamech, who boasted about murdering someone who merely hit him, the revenge of the ungodly is "seventy-sevenfold" (Gen. 4:24). But God's people do the math in a different way. When we are sinned against—even repeatedly—we bear with others and forgive them "seventy-seven times" (Matt. 18:22). As many times as an ungodly person would have struck out in revenge, a Christian reaches out in love.

This life of patience, says Paul, is conduct "worthy of the calling to which you have been called." God calls us to salvation, and behavior that is "worthy of the calling" is not, of course, behavior that *merits* this calling. Instead, it is behavior *shaped by* our calling and behavior that therefore *glorifies* the One who called us. When people who belong to Christ act like people who belong to Christ, we exalt Christ in the world. While our ungodly neighbors may snap at every offense, God's patient people work hard to bear with others, maintaining "the unity of the Spirit in the bond of peace"—and magnifying the gospel as we do.

Reflect: Are you surprised when people sin against you? How might your response to mistreatment change if you assumed mistreatment would be a regular part of your life and prepared in advance to respond?

Reflect: Read 1 Corinthians 13. How has Christ demonstrated love toward you that is "patient and kind" and "not irritable or resentful"? Ask him to produce this kind of love—one that "bears all things" and "endures all things"—in your heart.

Act: Think about an interaction today where someone is likely to sin against you: a rude coworker, a thoughtless church member, a grumpy neighbor. Prepare ahead of time for how you will respond patiently when you are mistreated.

DAY 4

Patience Is Slowness to Anger

Let every person be quick to hear, slow to speak, slow to anger; for the anger of man does not produce the righteousness of God. (James 1:19–20)

CAN YOU RELATE to Jonah? His story of weathering storms at sea and sloshing around in the belly of a fish might not mirror your own life history, but his impatience may. Jonah was not a man who waited around to see what God might do. Jonah was a man who reacted—and reacted quickly. When God called him to preach to Nineveh, he "made haste to flee" in the opposite direction (Jonah 4:2). When God demonstrated kindness toward the repentant Ninevites, Jonah was immediately and "exceedingly" angry (v. 1). When his wilted shade plant left him baking in the sun, Jonah demanded instant death (see v. 8). Jonah felt deeply, acted rashly, and spoke angrily. Can you relate?

Today's verse is a corrective to the Jonah in each of our hearts, and in it we see that one important aspect of patience is being slow to anger. Especially in the face of adversity, none of us naturally slows down. When someone mistreats us, we want to protest immediately. When our life circumstances are hard, we want to know how quickly things will get better. When work or relationships feel stagnant, we want change *now*. Not so fast, says James. Bite your tongue. Take your time. Wait and see.

Wisdom and slowness to anger are connected, as Proverbs explains: "Whoever is slow to anger has great understanding, but he who has a hasty temper exalts folly" (14:29). Slowness is not about speaking and acting at a snail's pace. It's about speaking and acting at the *right* pace.

It's also important to note that James doesn't forbid speaking and anger altogether. Throughout Scripture, we see instances when God's people—and even Christ himself—spoke boldly and demonstrated appropriate anger (see 1 Kings 21:17–24; Ps. 31:6; Luke 19:45–46; Gal. 3:1). There may be circumstances in which anger is right; there are many more in which it is not. James tells us we will have to slow down to determine which is which.

When we feel angry, giving vent to our anger often brings a temporary sense of satisfaction. But God comes to us, as he did to Jonah, and asks, "Do you do well to be angry?" (Jonah 4:4). James, also, urges us to take the long view and consider whether our hasty anger will "produce the righteousness of God." God himself is "slow to anger and abounding in steadfast love" (Ex. 34:6; Jonah 4:2), and when we are patient, we become like him. An immediate outburst may feel like it accomplishes something, but treading cautiously when we feel angry produces a bountiful harvest of righteousness.

Reflect: Why does it often feel satisfying to give immediate vent to anger? How is "the righteousness of God" a motivator of patience?

Reflect: Read Jonah 4:1–11 and Job 40:3–5. What's the difference between Jonah's and Job's responses to adversity? Are you more often like Jonah or Job? Ask the Lord to give you the spirit of Job.

Act: In the above verses, Job placed his hand over his mouth to keep himself from speaking rashly to God. Often, a physical cue is helpful to reinforce our spiritual priorities: we bow our heads in prayer to remind ourselves that we are humbly approaching God; we greet other Christians with a sign of affection (see Rom. 16:16) to remind ourselves that we love one another. Choose a physical gesture to remind you to speak and act slowly: take a deep breath, bite your tongue, or fold your hands.

WHY WAIT?

Patience is not easy, and the world around us offers little incentive to slow down. Thankfully, the Bible provides us with abundant motivation. Over the next few days, we'll allow ourselves to be compelled by what God says about why we should wait.

DAY 5

God Is Patient

The Lord passed before him and proclaimed, "The Lord, the Lord, a God merciful and gracious, slow to anger, and abounding in steadfast love and faithfulness." (Ex. 34:6)

"Thank you for your patience." The reply from my out-of-office coworker landed in my inbox almost as soon as I had clicked send on my email to her. From her beach blanket under the palm trees, she couldn't anticipate how her contacts would respond to a two-week delay, but her message indicated that patience would be a good choice. This kind of praise for patience seems to be nearly universal. "Thanks for being patient," the store clerk says when you finally reach the front of a long line. "Sorry about that. Thanks for waiting," the medical receptionist tells you over the phone at the end of a ten-minute hold. Most people know it's only right to refrain from causing a scene over a temporary delay.

But while most people instinctively acknowledge the moral correctness of patience, only people who know God can understand the true value of waiting well. In today's verse, the Lord displays the foundation for all human patience: his own patience. A few verses earlier, Moses asked the Lord, "Please show me now your ways, that I may know you in order to find favor in your sight" (Ex. 33:13). Moses was asking God to reveal his essence, his character, his name (see v. 19). And one thing God revealed was patience.

The fact that God is patient ("slow to anger") teaches us two important truths about patience. First, patience is good. God prefaces his self-revelation with these words: "I will make all my goodness pass before you" (Ex. 33:19). The God who is eternally and entirely good is patient with his people. The God who never

25

sins is always slow to anger. As we encounter difficult delays and frustrating people, we can be certain that choosing patience is choosing what is good.

The second truth about God's patience—and our own—is that patience is glorious. Moses asked God, "Please show me your glory" (Ex. 33:18; see also v. 22), and God showed that he is patient. In our world, patience often seems like a small thing, an insignificant virtue practiced mainly by the downtrodden and weak. It seems like something you do when you don't have a choice, when you are the hapless victim of circumstances or people more powerful than you. But this verse shows us that patience is much more magnificent than we might expect. The sovereign God of the universe clothes himself in patience and calls it his glory. And if it is the glory of God to be slow to anger, it is our glory too (see Prov. 19:11).

Being perfunctorily thanked for your patience by a retail employee doesn't make waiting well seem terribly glamorous. But, as today's verse shows us, patience is Godlike. When we are "slow to anger," we learn about God's character, practice his ways, and seek to please him. We have experienced God's patience toward us, and as we exercise patience, we imitate our great God. There's no better incentive to wait.

Reflect: Do you usually think of being patient as a significant act? Why or why not?

Reflect: Read Psalm 106. Notice how often God's people act faithlessly toward him. Notice how often he responds with restraint and mercy. Notice how his patience becomes a reason for Israel to praise him.

Act: When someone thanks you for your patience today, remind yourself that even small moments of waiting well are a way that we imitate our good and glorious God.

DAY 6

God Commands Patience

Put on then, as God's chosen ones, holy and beloved, compassionate
hearts, kindness, humility, meekness, and patience. (Col. 3:12)

IF YOU WERE to drive down my street, you'd see evidence
of children. Their basketball hoops and trampolines shape the
neighborhood topography; their tricycles and toys lie in yards
and driveways. On nice days, the kids themselves are outside:
riding skateboards, playing hide-and-seek, or returning from the
farm stand clutching a double scoop of black raspberry. Any driver
should know to proceed with caution. But, halfway down the
street, the city posted a prominent yellow sign: "Go Slow: Children." It might seem obvious that drivers shouldn't speed with
kids around, but they still need the law written out: "Go Slow."

Most of us acknowledge that we should be patient with the
circumstances and people around us. But, like late-for-work drivers in a neighborhood filled with kindergartners, we still need the
clear proclamation in today's verse: "Put on . . . patience." This
command, like all God's commands, is for our good. By it, he
teaches us his will, showing us what we should do. By it, he also
exposes our sin, showing us where we do wrong. For believers,
God's command ultimately points us to Christ as we seek forgiveness and help to obey.[1] Even if we think we already know it, being
told to proceed carefully is a message we need to hear.

God's command to patience also comes with an explanation
to motivate us. Yesterday we saw that patience is both good and
glorious. Today's verse shows us that patience is a mark of holiness. Because we are "God's chosen ones, holy and beloved," we
ought to act in ways that are consistent with who we are. By his
death and resurrection, Christ paid the penalty for our sins and

secured our righteousness. By giving us his Spirit, he sets us apart to himself and gives us a new heart. Because of Christ's work on our behalf, we are holy.[2] As his holy people, then, we must pursue holiness. We think and act in holy ways not to earn our salvation—as if we could!—but because our salvation compels us to live out our new identity in Christ. Since we are "holy and beloved," we "put on" holy and loving conduct. We care for others. We treat them with gentleness. We hold our own preferences loosely, and we acknowledge our own sin. We cultivate patience with the weak and suffer long with our enemies.

As we go about our lives, it's easy to rush impatiently toward our own goals without considering the good of other people. We can thoughtlessly ignore, dismiss, or mistreat others in our hurry to get what we want. But God lovingly places his command to patience in our path as a warning and a reminder: You are holy. Proceed carefully.

Reflect: Why do speed limit signs, flashing caution lights, and signaling construction workers have an effect on your actions? Can you think of other times when you take care because someone tells you to?

Reflect: Read Psalm 119:97–104. Give thanks to God for giving you his command to be patient. Acknowledge the blessings of living under God's law. Praise God for warning you away from "every evil way" (v. 101). Ask God to make his words about patience "sweeter than honey" to you (v. 103).

Act: Write out the command in today's verse ("put on . . . patience") and post it somewhere you will see it frequently: your vehicle dashboard, your bathroom mirror, or your computer screen.

DAY 7

God's People Have
Always Been Patient

*These all died in faith, not having received the things promised, but
having seen them and greeted them from afar, and having acknowledged
that they were strangers and exiles on the earth. (Heb. 11:13)*

EVERY DECEMBER, the Taylor University student body has an opportunity to wait. At the semester's final basketball game, students and alumni fill the stands in complete silence. After the tip-off, the stadium remains eerily quiet; layups, fouls, dunks, and steals elicit no response from the crowd. The tradition, known as "Silent Night," requires fans to wait through the early ups and downs of the game until a Taylor player scores the team's tenth point. When that ball finally sails through the hoop, thousands of Trojan fans break the silence, erupting into wild celebration. For generations of students, being a Taylor Trojan has meant being patient.

Today's verse reminds us that waiting is a common experience for God's people. "These all" refers to Hebrews 11's generation-spanning list of faithful men and women: Abel, Enoch, Noah, Abraham, Sarah, Isaac, Jacob, Joseph, Moses, Moses's parents, Rahab, Gideon, Barak, Samson, Jephthah, David, Samuel, and the prophets. "These all" waited with patience in life's circumstances. "These all" experienced hardship—often extreme hardship—while they waited. "These all" exercised exemplary faith despite the fact that they "did not receive what was promised" (v. 39) in this life.

If we belong to Christ, waiting patiently is part of our identity as well. Like the saints of Hebrews 11, we wait for God to act in a variety of circumstances, some temporal and some eternal. We long to add children to our families, and we long for God to establish his covenant family. We want our daily work to be fruitful, and we want God to cultivate fruit in his spiritual kingdom. We desire an end to our own physical suffering, and we desire God to end all suffering. In this life, we may see some answers to our prayers, but, like the saints of old, we wait for the ultimate fulfillment of God's purposes in eternity.

Thankfully, we don't have to wait alone. Our shared identity with God's people means we belong to a vast company of saints who have also exercised patience one day at a time. The people in Hebrews 11 form the "great . . . cloud of witnesses" who encourage us to wait with hope, "looking to Jesus" (Heb. 12:1–2). They experienced the difficulty of waiting, and now they have tasted its reward. What's more, we are surrounded by faithful men and women in our own churches who are waiting well. They are our brothers and sisters in patient endurance (see Rev. 1:9), pointing us to Christ as we wait. And, alongside them, we will one day rejoice as we together take possession of that final, heavenly country.

Reflect: Think of an example of how belonging to a group sometimes requires you to be patient: waiting with friends to be seated at a restaurant, waiting with your church for an answer to prayer, waiting with family members for news of a baby's birth. How does waiting alongside others make the wait better?

Reflect: Choose one of the saints mentioned in Hebrews 11 and read his or her narrative in the Old Testament. Consider what his or her story can teach you. Remind yourself that you don't wait alone; you belong to a vast company of God's patient people.

Act: In what area are you struggling to wait? Think of someone in your church who is also waiting—perhaps in similar circumstances. Ask that person if he or she would be willing to get together with you to pray for and encourage one another.

DAY 8

God Uses Your Patience to Bless Others

*To write the same things to you is no trouble to
me and is safe for you. (Phil. 3:1)*

THE APOSTLE PAUL knew all about repeating himself. As he
traveled throughout the known world, preaching sermons, plant-
ing churches, and writing letters, he told and retold the gospel
message. Only heaven will reveal exactly how many times Paul
proclaimed "Christ and him crucified" (1 Cor. 2:2). In particular
churches, he also had to review lessons that congregations had
forgotten or ignored—or that were especially important. With
the Corinthians, he repeated the basics of the Christian faith (see
1 Cor. 3:1–2). With the Galatians, he issued multiple warnings
against listening to false teachers (see Gal. 1:9). And with the
Philippians, he commanded them four times in the space of four
chapters to "rejoice!" (Phil. 2:18; 3:1; twice in 4:4). Paul's letters
are filled with things he had already said.

Like Paul, most of us have relationships that require us to proceed carefully, to lend a hand, to go slowly, and, sometimes, to
repeat ourselves. Mothers of toddlers, supervisors of new hires,
and caregivers for aging adults can especially relate. But whatever
the particular dynamics of our relationships, we can learn from
Paul's patient example.

First, Paul says in today's verse that repeating himself to the
Philippians is "no trouble." This is surprising. Our impatience usually stems from the fact that being patient seems like a great deal
of trouble. But Paul shows us that out of love for our neighbors,
being patient should not be an imposition. Jacob labored seven

years for Rachel, and "they seemed to him but a few days because of the love he had for her" (Gen. 29:20). Paul yearned for the Philippians "with the affection of Christ Jesus" (Phil. 1:8), so it didn't bother him to repeat himself a few times. We ought to value other people so much that going slowly on their behalf is no big deal.

Next, Paul says that his repeated exhortation is "safe for you." Paul recognized that he could do great good to the Philippians simply by being patient with them. Similarly, our patient words to others can encourage their hearts, equip them with truth, spur them to obedience, and point them to Christ. When Priscilla and Aquila took Apollos aside and patiently instructed him, the church gained a powerful apologist who "greatly helped" the believers in Achaia (Acts 18:27). God can use our patience to bless the entire church.

Ultimately, the ministry of Paul mirrors that of Jesus, of whom Isaiah prophesied, "a bruised reed he will not break, and a faintly burning wick he will not quench" (42:3). If God had not been long-suffering with us, we would have been instantly consumed by his wrath. But, as it is, our Lord has borne patiently with us: forgiving our sins, giving his Spirit to us, hearing our prayers, and instructing us in his Word again and again. He has done all these things as if they were "no trouble" to him because they are safe for us, his beloved people. Having received the blessing of his patience, can we not be patient with others?

Reflect: Think of a time when someone had to repeat themselves for your sake. How did you benefit from their patience?

Reflect: Read Acts 18:24–28. Notice how Priscilla and Aquila's patience was a blessing to Apollos and to the wider church. Consider who God might bless through your patience.

Act: Memorize Philippians 3:1. Call it to mind when you hear yourself saying the same things again to someone.

DAY 9

God Rewards Patience

Blessed is the man who remains steadfast under trial, for when
he has stood the test he will receive the crown of life, which
God has promised to those who love him. (James 1:12)

IN OUR DAILY LIVES, we are familiar with rewards. If I make
enough purchases, my credit card company rewards me with air-
line miles. If I work hard enough at my job, my employer rewards
me with a raise. If my children read enough books over the sum-
mer, the local library rewards them with an ice cream cone. But
in each of these examples, the "reward" is really a payment. If we
fulfill the terms, we get something good.

The Bible talks about reward too. But when Scripture tells us
"the righteous are rewarded with good" (Prov. 13:21), it means
something different than a prize for good behavior. In the first
place, our actions are never perfectly righteous. Even our best
efforts are infected by sin, fall far short of perfect holiness, and
deserve God's wrath. And, in the second place, God doesn't
owe us anything. He is the Creator and we are his creatures, and
nothing we do can place him in our debt. In biblical terms, then,
reward is based solely on our acceptance in Christ (the only perfectly righteous man) and is bestowed purely according to God's
kindness. Because of Christ, God is pleased with us and gives us
good things even when our own efforts are weak and imperfect.[1]

Knowing this, we can understand—and rejoice in!—the
assertion from today's verse that God rewards patience. James
wrote to a church that was tempted to give up under "trials of
various kinds" and the "testing of [its] faith" (1:2–3). In response,
the apostle reminded the believers that trials and testing are God-
given opportunities to learn patient endurance (see v. 3). And he

33

encouraged them that their steadfastness would one day receive a reward: "the crown of life, which God has promised to those who love him." Those first-century Christians, following in the steps of Moses, endured by "looking to the reward" (Heb. 11:26).

Like the members of the early church, we are often tempted to quit. Sickness and suffering and doubt and discouragement pursue us daily. Giving up sounds easy. Patient endurance seems like a long, hard road that stretches out in front of us forever. But James's encouragement to the early church is an encouragement to us too. When we remain steadfast in the faith, we will discover that God has always been faithful toward us. Even our patience will be revealed as the work of his Spirit in us. On the last day, we will not be ashamed, and we will not be disappointed (see Ps. 25:3). Instead, the promised "crown of life" will make our years of endurance worth the wait. The Lord will crown us with glory, bless us with eternal life, and publicly declare our love for him and his love for us.

Dear Christian, look to the reward.

Reflect: What is one area where you currently need to practice patient endurance? Do you ever think about the reward that awaits? Why or why not?

Reflect: Read Hebrews 11:24–28. How did "looking to the reward" motivate Moses to bear up patiently under affliction?

Act: When you meet "trials of various kinds" and "the testing of your faith" today, remind yourself that you will not have to be patient forever. One day, God will give you the "crown of life."

CULTIVATING PATIENCE BY LOOKING TO CHRIST

Do you want a model of patience to imitate? Better yet, do you want a sympathetic friend and powerful ally who comes alongside you as you wait? Christ is all those things, and over the next few days, we will meditate on him and learn patience from him.

DAY 10

Christ, Our Example

For to this you have been called, because Christ also
suffered for you, leaving you an example, so that you might follow
in his steps. . . . When he was reviled, he did not revile in return;
when he suffered, he did not threaten, but continued entrusting
himself to him who judges justly. (1 Peter 2:21, 23)

"I'M NOT EXACTLY sure what a patient parent looks like," my friend told me. "My home growing up was so tense. I never knew when my parents were going to explode. Now, I struggle to know how to be patient with my kids." Like my friend, many of us feel the lack of role models as we seek to practice patience. If we haven't had a patient employer, a patient neighbor, a patient teacher, or a patient roommate, it's hard to know how to be patient when we assume those roles ourselves.

Thankfully, God hasn't left us without an example. In sending the Son to take on human flesh, to live a life of perfect obedience, and to die a sinless death on the cross, he gave us the greatest— and most helpful—example of patience we could ever want. As we seek to cultivate patience in our own lives, we can begin by looking to Christ.

In today's verses we see, first, that as a human person living in a fallen world among sinful people, Christ knew all the struggles of life. Like us, he was hungry, tired, and thirsty (see Matt. 4:2; 8:24; John 19:28). He had to bear patiently with accusatory Pharisees, slow-witted disciples, and unjust government rulers. He, like us, was tempted to give up and to lash out. Wherever you struggle, Christ has been there before you.

Today's verses also tell us that Jesus sets us an example in how he responded to mistreatment: "When he was reviled, he did not revile in return; when he suffered, he did not threaten." Every day, in every kind of circumstance, Christ was patient. Even in his most extreme suffering, Jesus acted with perfect patience: "He was oppressed, and he was afflicted, yet he opened not his mouth; like a lamb that is led to the slaughter, and like a sheep that before its shearers is silent, so he opened not his mouth" (Isa. 53:7).

Finally, we see the foundation for his patience: Christ clung to hope. In the ordinary sufferings of daily life on earth, and in the extraordinary suffering of his atoning death on the cross, Christ did not succumb to impatience because he "continued entrusting himself to him who judges justly." Dear Christian, we have the same hope. One day, God will judge all wrongs, set all things right, restore what has been lost, and renew what has been damaged. Your Savior waited patiently for that day. Follow in his steps.

Reflect: Have you ever walked through deep snow or hiked a thickly wooded trail? How does that experience become easier when you have someone in front of you stomping down the snow or holding back the branches? How does following in Christ's steps encourage you?

Reflect: Read Matthew 26:47–68. How did Christ display patience as he faced the greatest suffering anyone has ever experienced? How does his example give you courage to be patient in your own trials?

Act: The local church is an excellent place to find examples of patience. Identify someone in your congregation who displays Christlike patience in the circumstances of his or her life. Ask that person to share how the Spirit has helped him or her.

DAY 11

Christ, Our Sympathetic Friend

*Then Jesus was led up by the Spirit in the wilderness
to be tempted by the devil. And after fasting forty days
and forty nights, he was hungry. (Matt. 4:1–2)*

"A SILLY IDEA is current that good people do not know what
temptation means," wrote C. S. Lewis in *Mere Christianity*. "This
is an obvious lie. Only those who try to resist temptation know
how strong it is. After all, you find out the strength of the Ger-
man army by fighting against it, not by giving in. You find out the
strength of a wind by trying to walk against it, not by lying down.
A man who gives in to temptation after five minutes simply does
not know what it would have been like an hour later."[1]

In the fight against impatience, we might not think of Jesus
as a sympathetic friend. After all, he lived his entire earthly life
without once snapping at his coworkers, grumbling in a slow-
moving crowd, questioning God's timing, or griping about the
ignorance of his neighbors. Unlike us, from infancy to the day
of his death, Jesus always resisted the temptation to sin. But, as
Lewis points out, this makes Christ the most understanding
friend we could have.

At the beginning of his earthly ministry, Christ was led into
the wilderness by the Spirit "to be tempted by the devil." You and
I usually come into temptation by our folly—our "own desire"
lures and entices us into the wilderness (James 1:14). But Christ's
perfect righteousness gave Satan no opportunity for a chance
encounter. He had to make an appointment. At the arranged place
and time, Satan came prepared with every tool at his disposal.

Jesus was weary and weak after forty days without food, and
Satan's first maneuver was to tempt him to instant gratification:

"Command these stones to become loaves of bread," he told our Lord (Matt. 4:3). Why trust God to give what is best? Why look for satisfaction beyond your immediate desires? Why rest in God's perfect timing? Why wait a moment longer? Alone in the wilderness, our Lord met the full force of Satan's pressure. He withstood temptation far beyond what any of us has borne, to the point of shedding his blood (see Heb. 12:3–4). While we often give in to temptation after only moments, Christ resisted for a lifetime.

Just as he did with Christ, Satan regularly waves fast food in front of hungry people and suggests that giving in to impatience is only reasonable. Why trust God in your singleness, your childlessness, your unemployment, your hard relationships, your temporary inconvenience? Why wait a moment longer? Although these temptations are extremely difficult, they are not unique to us. We have a divine friend seated in heaven who understands our temptation and who encourages us never to give in.

Reflect: We sometimes assume that someone who is happy is naive, that someone who is content must also be ignorant, and that someone who is faithful just comes by it naturally. How does the Lewis quote at the beginning of today's devotional change your thinking about someone in your life who exhibits patience?

Reflect: Read Hebrews 4:14–16. Give thanks to God that you have a divine friend who understands the temptations you face. Boldly ask for his help to cultivate patience.

Act: Think of someone in your life—a child, an elderly relative, a friend—who also struggles with impatience. Sympathize with him or her about the difficulty of resisting Satan's temptation. Commit to bringing one another to Christ in prayer.

DAY 12

Christ, Our Power

Let us run with endurance the race that is set before us, looking to Jesus, the founder and perfecter of our faith. (Heb. 12:1–2)

"I CAN'T WAIT!" This cheerful expression of anticipation is a common part of our lives. We text it to friends when confirming weekend plans, say it to coworkers about our upcoming vacations, and hear it repeatedly from children throughout the month of December. It's followed by smiles, and it's meant figuratively; we don't seriously think we can't wait for a day at the beach or gifts under the tree. But sometimes "I can't wait" takes a more frantic tone. Faced with unwanted singleness, financial insecurity, prolonged illness, or relational upheaval, we feel desperate for a resolution. Although we might not say it aloud, "I can't wait!" becomes the sincere cry of our hearts. We really can't wait. Or, at least, we can't wait well.

Most of us know we should be patient. We even know the practical steps we should take to cultivate patience: Take a deep breath. Read Scripture. Pray more. Worry less. Trust God. Adjust expectations. The Lord clearly commands us to "put on . . . patience" (Col. 3:12), and when we become impatient, we do feel guilty. But, again and again, we have to admit that knowing we *ought* to be patient doesn't mean we can do it.

Thankfully, the good news of the gospel is not simply that Christ tells us to be patient, or even that he sets us an example of a patient life, but also that he is at work in us to make us patient. As we see in today's verses, impatient people can look to Christ for help. He is the "founder and perfecter of our faith," and we run the race of faith with the endurance he gives us.

Christ works patience in us in several ways. Christ's work on the cross frees us from the tyranny of sin and frees us to practice righteousness (see Rom. 6:5–14). Because of Christ, we do not have to be impatient. Christ also gives us his Spirit. The Spirit lives in us, convicting us of sin and spurring us to godliness, continually helping us to cultivate a life of patience (see Gal. 5:16–24). Finally, Christ prays for us. The writer to the Hebrews says that "he is able to save to the uttermost those who draw near to God through him, since he always lives to make intercession for them" (Heb. 7:25). Just as Christ prayed for Peter before his temptation (see Luke 22:31–32), he is now praying for us to attain patience.[1]

On our own, we can't wait. But we don't have to grit our teeth and practice patience in our own strength. We "run with endurance the race that is set before us" because we are looking to Jesus. He founded our faith and is perfecting our faith. He conquered sin's mastery, gives us his own patient endurance (see Rev. 1:9), and continually prays for us. In Christ, we have everything we need.

Reflect: What is something in your life that makes you sincerely think "I can't wait"?

Reflect: Read Galatians 5:16–24. Thank God for sending the indwelling Spirit to produce the fruit of patience in your life. Ask him to help you to "[crucify] the flesh" (v. 24) and "walk by the Spirit" (v. 16).

Act: Think of a recent time when you exercised patience— even for a moment. Give thanks for this evidence of Christ's powerful work in you. Be encouraged that "he who began a good work in you will bring it to completion" (Phil. 1:6).

DAY 13

Christ's Glory, Our Hope

For the grace of God has appeared ... training us to renounce
ungodliness and worldly passions, and to live self-controlled,
upright, and godly lives in the present age, waiting for our
blessed hope, the appearing of the glory of our great
God and Savior Jesus Christ. (Titus 2:11–13)

IF YOU'VE EVER taken a long airplane flight, you know how easy it is to become impatient. After the flurry of boarding and the initial amusement of selecting snack and drinks, there's not much to do. Cocooned in the stale air and thrumming engine noise with only clouds or darkness visible through the windows, you may be traveling at five hundred miles an hour, but it feels like you are at a standstill. Even after hours of flying, the tiny airplane icon on the flight tracker has moved mere inches. You're eager to get to your destination, but it's hard to believe you are making any progress.

In many of life's circumstances, we become impatient when we don't see results. We bear with difficult people, and they continue to be difficult. We persevere under trials, and we only encounter new trials. It's tough to be patient when it seems like nothing is changing. But that's often because we are looking for change in the wrong place. Today's verses reorient our focus. As we wait on him, God is producing change in *us* and will one day bring about our complete transformation.

First, Paul writes that we are being changed now. As we persevere in the faith, God's grace is at work in us to kill sin and cultivate righteousness. Elsewhere, Paul says that "we all, with unveiled face, beholding the glory of the Lord, are being transformed into the same image from one degree of glory to another" (2 Cor. 3:18). Although our progress might not be obvious, we are slowly and steadily becoming more like Christ with every day we walk with him.

But that's not all. Paul also encourages us by telling us that one day we will be completely changed forever. Our waiting as Christians is not ultimately for a change in our earthly circumstances; we are waiting for the coming of Christ. And at exactly the right time, Christ will appear, and we will share in his glory (see 1 Peter 1:7–9; 5:1, 4). We will see him as he is, we will be made like him, and we will lay our crowns in worship at his feet (see 1 John 3:2; Rev. 4:10).

This gives us hope. While we are often tempted to practice patience grudgingly, the Lord reminds us that we are "waiting for our blessed hope" (Titus 2:13) and our hope "does not put us to shame" (Rom. 5:5). We can wait patiently—even joyfully!—because we know that the end of our waiting is both certain and glorious. Christ will one day return, and he will change everything.

Christian, we have no greater hope.

Reflect: Regarding patience, Jen Wilkin writes, "We [might] overlook the possibility that the waiting itself could be the good and perfect gift, delivered right to our doorstep."[1] In what ways could waiting be a good gift from God?

Reflect: Read 2 Timothy 4:7–8. What does it mean to love Christ's appearing? Do you look as eagerly for Christ's return as you do for an end to your temporary troubles? Ask God to give you a heart set on Christ's coming.

Act: Make a list of some specific ways God has changed you through seasons of waiting. How are you more like Christ because you have had to exercise patience?

CULTIVATING PATIENCE
BY UNDERSTANDING TIME

"I don't have time for this!" is the frantic cry of our impatient hearts. But, over the next few days, we'll see that time is not under our control. Instead, God appoints each minute of our lives for our good and his glory.

DAY 14

Time Is Short

You also, be patient. Establish your hearts, for the coming of the Lord is at hand. Do not grumble against one another, brothers and sisters, so that you may not be judged; behold, the Judge is standing at the door. (James 5:8–9)

THE WHITE RABBIT in Lewis Carroll's *Alice in Wonderland* is famously short on time. Having been summoned by the Queen of Hearts, he dashes in and out of the story, repeatedly checking his pocket watch and telling Alice how late he is. The white rabbit is not a very appealing character. From the tips of his ears to his fluffy white tail, he is entirely self-absorbed. He can't even manage a polite greeting to Alice as he scampers past, let alone help the poor girl to find her way.

Often, like the white rabbit, we are so focused on the shortness of time that we allow ourselves to fall into impatience. The unexpected traffic, the tardy employee, the dawdling child all cause our hearts to explode, "Hurry up! I don't have much time!" But in today's verses, James gives counterintuitive wisdom about time: because it is short, we should be patient.

First, James tells us, time is much shorter than we think. We may be rushing around to finish that project or get to that appointment, but we have set our eyes on an ultimately insignificant deadline. What's more, we assume our earthly deadlines will just keep coming due, one after another. But the real deadline—the end of all things—is coming much faster than we think. The Bible tells us the day of the Lord is "coming soon" (Rev. 22:20), it is "at hand" (1 Peter 4:7), and it is "near" (Heb. 10:25). Time, Scripture says, is "very short" (1 Cor. 7:29). While we are busy manipulating entries in our Google calendars, the end is almost upon us.

Next, James tells us, judgment is certain. The last day is not a flexible deadline—open to requests for an extension. The day is "coming" even now. And it will not be impersonal—it won't be like filing your taxes or scheduling an automated system reboot. At the end of days, the Judge himself will appear. The Lord—who is today "standing at the door"—will personally come to pass sentence on everyone who has ever lived.

Perhaps counterintuitively, these truths ought to increase our patience. On the one hand, the shortness of time ought to make us rightly fear God and seek to obey him. We cannot waste time in impatient unrighteousness, squandering our moments in anger and anxiety, and be found grumbling when the Judge appears. On the other hand, the shortness of time ought to give us courage. In the face of his sure return, we "establish [our] hearts." One day very soon, our Lord will right all wrongs and judge all injustices. Be patient. He is coming.

Reflect: When you are running late, how do you feel? How do you treat others around you? Why does the shortness of time often tempt you to sin?

Reflect: Read Genesis 29:1–30. Notice how Jacob's love for Rachel shaped his understanding of time and fueled his willingness to work patiently for many years. Christians are those who "have loved [Christ's] appearing" (2 Tim. 4:8), so how should this love shape our view of time?

Act: Every time you look at a clock today, remind yourself that time is short. Every hour that passes brings the day of the Lord's coming closer. Allow the ticking seconds to encourage you to establish your heart.

DAY 15

Afflictions Are Temporary

For the Lord will not cast off forever, but, though he
cause grief, he will have compassion according to the
abundance of his steadfast love. (Lam. 3:31–32)

LIKE JESUS BEFORE HIM, Paul was acquainted with suffering. He was beaten, stoned, and shipwrecked multiple times (see 2 Cor. 11:24–25). He was "afflicted . . . perplexed . . . persecuted . . . [and] struck down . . . always carrying in the body the death of Jesus" (2 Cor. 4:8–10). He was in constant danger: from evildoers, from natural disasters, and even from some who claimed the name of Christ (see 2 Cor. 11:26). He was frequently hungry, thirsty, and cold (see 2 Cor. 11:27). He faced "afflictions, hardships, calamities, beatings, imprisonments, riots, labors, [and] sleepless nights" (2 Cor. 6:4–5). He even experienced a thorn in the flesh, "a messenger of Satan," that never left him (2 Cor. 12:7). Paul suffered greatly. And yet, in the same letter where he details these sufferings, Paul called his troubles a "light momentary affliction" (2 Cor. 4:17).

Light and *momentary* are probably not the first words we'd choose to describe our own afflictions. Whether we have a cold or cancer, we often groan under hardships as if they will never let up. We grow impatient when we believe that things will always be as difficult as they are at this moment. We often forget the divine promise that Paul undoubtedly knew: "The Lord will not cast off forever." As today's verses remind us, afflictions—no matter how unrelenting they may seem—are temporary.

Surprisingly, Jeremiah's lament is unapologetic about the fact that our trials come from God's hand. "The Lord" is the one who casts us off, and he is the one who causes grief. This should humble us before him; it should also give us comfort. Because he is both sovereign and abundantly loving toward us, the Lord will put an end to our suffering at exactly the right moment. The one who casts off is also the one who "will have compassion." We have God's promise that our trials will not last forever, and all his promises are sure.

What's more, our temporary trials will give way to eternal praise: "You have turned for me my mourning into dancing; you have loosed my sackcloth and clothed me with gladness, that my glory may sing your praise and not be silent. O LORD my God, I will give thanks to you forever!" (Ps. 30:11–12). We can be patient under affliction today, waiting confidently for the time when our sorrow will turn to joy forever.

Reflect: Medical professionals often preface uncomfortable treatments with "This will just be a quick pinch" or "This will be over soon, I promise." Why is it easier to bear something you know won't last long?

Reflect: Read Genesis 17:15–21. What does verse 17 say Sarah's affliction was (see also Gen. 16:1)? How many years had she waited? According to the Lord, when would her trial be over? How is it comforting to you to know that God has already decided the exact moment when your afflictions will end?

Act: A friend of mine[1] urges suffering believers to take "the short view" and "the long view" of their trials, avoiding "the middle view" altogether. The middle view unhelpfully asks, "Can I still bear this trial next week or next month or next year?" The short view asks, "Can I bear this trial for today?" and the long view asks, "Can I bear this trial in light of eternity?" Where do you need to focus on the short and long view?

DAY 16

Human Souls Have Eternal Value

The Lord is not slow to fulfill his promise as some count slowness,
but is patient toward you, not wishing that any should perish,
but that all should reach repentance. (2 Peter 3:9)

OVER THE YEARS, each of my four children learned a catechism question that asks, "Have you a soul as well as a body?"
The answer catches at my heart every time I hear it: "Yes. I have a
soul that will never die."[1] Whether it's on the lips of a toddler or a
teen, this answer seems designed for the instruction of the parent
as much as for the child. No matter how badly the day has gone,
I find it's nearly impossible to be annoyed with any child when I
seriously contemplate the fact that his or her soul will last forever.

Often, we become impatient with other people because we fail
to recognize their significant and lasting value. When they linger
over getting dressed in the morning, procrastinate on important
projects, or require us to remind them—again!—about something that seems self-evident, we tend to view them as inconve-
niences. We become so focused on their actions in the moment
that we forget about their value in eternity. Today's verse, like the
children's catechism question, redirects us to take the long view
of the people around us. Our children and coworkers, friends and
neighbors are people who will either be judged or repent. Each
one of them has a soul that will never die.

Peter's words to the churches describe a God who is not
bothered by the passing of time if it means that people will be
eternally saved. Although it seemed to the first-century Christians that the Lord had forgotten about his promise to return,
Peter assured them that God is simply being patient. In his saving purposes for his elect people, the Lord counts time differently

than we do: "One day is as a thousand years, and a thousand years as one day" (2 Peter 3:8). Unlike us, God is not focused on the clock. He is focused on doing good to souls. And if delay means that people will "reach repentance," the Lord is willing to wait as long as it takes.

In our interactions with others, we should seek to mirror the patience of the God who has been patient with us. Even if people cause us trouble and do not readily repent, we must remind ourselves that they are image bearers created for God's purposes. Just as the Lord was not willing that we would perish, we must not be eager for them to come under God's wrath. Our temporary inconvenience may be gospel opportunity. And if we can do good for their souls, we must be patient. Other people may cost us valuable minutes, but their souls are worth all the time in the world.

Reflect: Think about a recent time when you became impatient with someone. How were you viewing that person in the moment? How might you have responded differently if you were intentionally looking out for his or her eternal good?

Reflect: Read Mark 10:17–22. What was Jesus doing when the man interrupted him? What misconceptions did the man have? What was Jesus's heart attitude toward the man? How would you describe Jesus's responses? Ask God to give you Christlike love and patience as you are interrupted, delayed, and misunderstood by others today.

Act: Today, when you have to wait on someone or bear with someone, tell yourself, "This person has a soul that will never die."

CULTIVATING PATIENCE BY UNDERSTANDING YOUR CIRCUMSTANCES

When trials come, it's tempting to focus on a single question: "When will this be over?" But in the next few days, we will adopt a wider perspective and seek to understand our difficult circumstances in light of God's eternal purposes.

DAY 17

God Has Been Patient with You

The steadfast love of the LORD never ceases; his mercies
never come to an end; they are new every morning;
great is your faithfulness. (Lam. 3:22–23)

ONE DAY, Jesus told his disciples a story (see Matt. 18:21–35). In a certain kingdom, there was a servant who owed the king an enormous debt—more money than the man could have earned in a thousand lifetimes. "Have patience with me," the servant begged the king, "and I will pay you everything" (v. 26). Graciously, the king went far beyond the servant's request; he forgave him his debt entirely. But the servant promptly went out and found a fellow servant who owed him a much smaller debt and demanded repayment. "Have patience with me," the second servant begged, "and I will pay you" (v. 29). The first man, unlike his merciful king, refused this plea and put the debtor in prison. When the king heard about it, he chastised his servant, "Should not you have had mercy on your fellow servant, as I had mercy on you?" (v. 33).

If you've been a Christian for any length of time, this parable is undoubtedly familiar, and even a child can understand its meaning. Unfortunately, though, when it comes to being patient with others, we often forget the lesson of Jesus's story. Like the unforgiving servant, we reckon our own debt to be small and imagine the debts of others to be beyond what we can be expected to bear.

Today's verses invite us to meditate on God's steadfast love— remembering just how patient the Lord has been with us. From the days of our births, he patiently sustained our lives as we walked in rebellion against him. At just the right time, he forgave all our sins and made us new creations in Christ, though we did nothing to deserve his kindness. And, to this day, loving us *still* requires much patience. Like Adam and Eve, we break the simplest and clearest of God's commands. Like the wandering Israelites, we grumble about our circumstances even when God has provided everything we really need. Like Jonah, we impetuously run away from God and then blame him when things don't go well. Like Peter, we fail to acknowledge the Lord, publicly denying him by our words and actions. Like the Corinthian church, we act like spiritual babies even though we have abundant resources for growth. Again and again, faced with our debts, we must come to the Lord and plead, "Have patience with me!"

And, as Lamentations sweetly tells us, he does. His covenant love for us "never ceases," no matter how grievous our sins. His forgiving and restoring mercies "never come to an end," no matter how many times we must draw on them. His grace toward us is "new every morning," as if the previous day's failures had not happened. His faithfulness is greater than we can imagine.

Shouldn't God's daily patience with us cause us to overflow in daily thanksgiving toward him?

> **Reflect:** List the ways that the Lord has been patient with you over the past twenty-four hours. Why do you think we are so quick to forget these mercies?
>
> **Reflect:** Read Ephesians 2:1–10. What were you like before God saved you? How did God show mercy and patience toward you? How does meditating on God's steadfast love increase your own love for him?
>
> **Act:** Before you head into a situation today where you likely will need to be patient with someone, remind yourself of how patient God has been with you.

DAY 18

Every Moment of Your Life Has Value

I perceived that whatever God does endures forever; nothing can be added to it, nor anything taken from it. God has done it, so that people fear before him. (Eccl. 3:14)

TRAFFIC JAMS ARE one of the modern world's mysteries. As you make your way down the road, the other cars unexpectedly slow to a crawl or come to a stop. Your phone's navigation adds thirty minutes to your ETA, and you wait. You queue another podcast. You jockey for position in a slightly less crowded lane. When you finally inch your way to the end of the bottleneck, you look around—expecting to see evidence of a recent accident or a construction zone. Instead, you see nothing. Behind you, cars stretch for miles. In front of you, the road opens wide. The last half hour suddenly seems pointless.

Like an unexplained traffic jam, waiting on the Lord often appears pointless. We fight against besetting sin, asking the Lord to give us decisive victory, only to face new temptations the next day. We plead with God for the fulfillment of unmet desires, looking for answers to our good requests, only to receive silence in reply. We work hard in the callings we have been given, only to harvest thorns and thistles. We endure for days and years, and we come away feeling like waiting on the Lord was all a waste of time.

Today's verse reminds us that every moment of our lives has value. Whether we are working or feasting, we are living under God's timetable (see Eccl. 3:9–13), and the events around us are something that "God does." This gives significance to every circumstance. The Most High God arranges your calendar. As the psalmist proclaimed, "In [God's] book were written, every one of them, the days that were formed for me, when as yet there was none of them" (Ps. 139:16).

And God's control over our days should give us comfort. Our God is all-wise and all-powerful; Solomon declares that "nothing can be added to [his work], nor anything taken from it." Because God rules over our lives, everything is exactly as it should be. And, despite how it may sometimes appear to us, nothing in our lives is wasted. "Whatever God does endures forever," and even seasons of waiting accomplish his gracious and eternal purposes.

Ultimately, these truths ought to draw us to worship. As we wait on the Lord, we learn to "fear before him"—to acknowledge our weakness and to trust his goodness. Like Job, we humble ourselves before God, confessing, "I know that you can do all things, and that no purpose of yours can be thwarted" (Job 42:2).

Reflect: John Piper famously wrote, "God is always doing 10,000 things in your life, and you may be aware of 3 of them."[1] How does remembering God's active, hidden work help you to be patient?

Reflect: Read 2 Corinthians 12:7–10. What was Paul's difficulty? What did Paul ask the Lord to do? What was the Lord's answer? How was suffering patiently under this trial necessary for Paul's good?

Act: As you survey your calendar for the coming days, take a moment to humbly acknowledge that God orders every moment of your life. The events on your schedule—and the unforeseen delays that are sure to occur—are all under his sovereign care and are all valuable to his purposes. Meditate on Proverbs 16:9: "The heart of man plans his way, but the LORD establishes his steps."

DAY 19

Trials Are the School of Patience

Count it all joy, my brothers and sisters, when you meet
trials of various kinds, for you know that the testing of
your faith produces steadfastness. (James 1:2–3)

"Don't pray for patience," you've probably heard someone say. "God just might take you up on it!" Behind our wry smiles and awkward chuckles is an uncomfortable truth: there is no easy way to learn patience.

Today's verses affirm that, for believers, trials are the school of patience. Under God's sovereign hand, the testing of our faith is a carefully chosen curriculum, designed by him to produce steadfastness in our hearts. Although we might endure difficulties hoping our circumstances will change, James reveals that the greatest change happens in us, even while we wait.

The Lord produces this steadfastness through trials of "various kinds," with each person's circumstances uniquely intended for his or her good. A recurring battle with sin is often his means of training us to renounce ungodliness (see Titus 2:11–13). Affliction allows us to learn that his power is made perfect in weakness (see 2 Cor. 12:9). Unmet desires may be his way of redirecting our desires toward himself (see Ps. 73:25–26). In hundreds of situations, the Lord teaches us patience through suffering.

However, trials don't produce patience in everyone. Only the "brothers and sisters" benefit from testing. Job's wife responded to hardship (the death of her children, the loss of her livelihood, the crushing of her husband) with impatience. "Curse God and die," she told Job (Job 2:9). Get out of your troubles as quickly as possible, no matter the cost to your soul. By contrast, Job submitted to the lessons of God's school—"the LORD gave, and the LORD has taken away; blessed be the name of the LORD" (Job 1:21)—and he emerged steadfast (see James 5:11). For the wicked, trials are simply an occasion for greater sin. For the righteous, trials produce righteousness.

In God's classroom, the course of study lasts for a lifetime. We draw on what we've learned in the past in order to endure present trials, and enduring today's trials teaches us further lessons in patience, equipping us for the future. In the school of patience, not a single minute of learning is a waste. The line at the drive-through prepares us for the wait in the cancer center. The five-minute delay with a toddler prepares us to suffer long with a teen. Every day, we grow in endurance even as we must exercise greater endurance. Steadfastness has "its full effect" in our hearts, making us "perfect and complete, lacking in nothing" (James 1:4).

Thus we can count the testing of our faith as a reason for joy. Although the trials themselves are difficult, God has good purposes in them. In fact, we can arrive at patience in no other way.

Reflect: What are some circumstances that the Lord has used to teach you patience in the past? Have you found it true that "there is no easy way to learn patience"?

Reflect: Read Job 19:9–27. List Job's various trials. Can you relate to any of Job's expressions of weariness and sorrow? What was Job's great hope (see vv. 25–27)? How did his trials prepare him to wait patiently for his Redeemer's appearing?

Act: Think about a time in your school days when you approached your studies with seriousness and diligence. Perhaps it was the first time your kindergarten teacher assigned homework or the day when you began the research for your PhD. As you encounter trials today, ask the Lord to remind you that they are his good school of patience and ask him to help you to learn well.

DAY 20

God Designs Your Circumstances for the Good of Your Soul

In this you rejoice, though now for a little while, if necessary, you have been grieved by various trials, so that the tested genuineness of your faith—more precious than gold that perishes though it is tested by fire—may be found to result in praise and glory and honor at the revelation of Jesus Christ. (1 Peter 1:6–7)

PRODUCTIVITY SEEMS TO be the buzzword of our era. Everywhere we look, podcasts, apps, and books promise to help us to do more. If we would just set a timer, turn off our phones, or buy a new planner—they assure us—we'll reach our goals and accomplish more in less time. Much of this advice is helpful. But secular counsel to "do more faster" can sometimes blind us to the fact that our circumstances are not, ultimately, under our control and our goals are not, ultimately, benchmarks we set for ourselves. When we believe we can plan every minute, impatience seizes its opportunity. Having to mop spilled milk under the high chair wasn't on our agenda, and so we overflow in sinful frustration.

Today's verses are a helpful encouragement to everyone whose days—and years—are different from what they had intended. Writing to a church under affliction, Peter declares that hard and unforeseen circumstances are not the random interruptions they appear to be. Instead, everything that happens to believers is exactly according to plan.

When events don't progress according to our schedule, we often assume that they aren't progressing according to any schedule. But we would be wrong. The "various" difficulties that come into our lives—as small as spilled milk and as large as terminal illness—are on God's precise timetable. They happen "now"—at this exact moment, a time carefully selected by God himself even before we were born—and they happen "for a little while," taking up only the space of time that our wise and sovereign God intends. Because God is gracious, our afflictions do not happen randomly, and they do not last indefinitely. Before you were even aware of that approaching trial, God had already decreed the exact minute of its end.

We can also take comfort in the fact that our loving heavenly Father knows the trials he sends are hard. Sometimes, we are even "grieved" by them. But he "does not afflict from his heart" (Lam. 3:33) and brings difficulties only "if necessary" (1 Peter 1:6) for the testing and perfecting of our faith. Our trials are not pointless, and, one day, they will produce better results than we can imagine: "Praise and glory and honor at the revelation of Jesus Christ."

With this perspective, we can resist the temptation to grumble or lash out when we don't accomplish everything we intend. Instead, we can make our plans for tomorrow contingent on "if the Lord wills" (James 4:15), trusting our hours and days—and our interruptions—to the One who promises that "for those who love God all things work together for good" (Rom. 8:28).

Reflect: How is seeking to be productive a good thing in your life? How can it sometimes be harmful?

Reflect: Read Matthew 9:18–26. Who interrupted Jesus? What was his attitude toward her? How did the interruption multiply opportunities for God's glory in this story? Do you think of interruptions in your life as additional chances to serve and praise God?

Act: When something (or someone) interrupts your plans for the day, turn to the Lord. Confess your frustration and ask him to help you to trust that he has good purposes for you.

WHAT TO DO
WHILE YOU WAIT

Although we sometimes think of patience as a slow twiddling of our spiritual thumbs in the silence of life's waiting room, patience isn't passive. Over the next few days, we'll learn how to redeem the time as we wait.

DAY 21

Do Good

Do not withhold good from those to whom it is due,
when it is in your power to do it. (Prov. 3:27)

SEVERAL YEARS AGO, a pizza chain featured an ad campaign guaranteeing that pizza orders would be delivered in under thirty minutes. Unfortunately, by putting pressure on delivery drivers to rush pizzas to customers, the company was accused of causing traffic incidents. In response, the chain created a new ad with the tagline "You Got 30 Minutes." While their pizza was in transit, people in the ads visited with friends or completed a workout. Instead of focusing on how quickly the drivers could deliver, the new commercials showed what customers could accomplish while they waited.[1]

Today's verse also moves our focus from how soon our circumstances might change to what we can accomplish while we wait. "[Make] the best use of the time," Paul wrote to the Ephesians (5:16). In the Christian life, not a moment can be squandered. Although a period of waiting can seem like a waste, today's verse exhorts us to look for opportunities to do good.

Especially when we are waiting on other people—an incompetent employee, a foot-dragging teenager, or a perpetually oblivious spouse—we face the temptation to become bitter toward them. We count every minute we've had to delay on their behalf, and we resent them for it. Our natural inclination is to "withhold good"—to stand by and watch them fail. But Solomon rebukes our pride. These moments are valuable opportunities to care for the people around us. Just as the Lord took the posture of a servant for our sake, we who look to him in faith ought to likewise humble ourselves for the good of others (see Phil. 2:3–8). While we wait, "How can I help you?" should be ready on our lips and in our hearts.

Waiting also often makes us weary and provides an easy excuse to retreat from well-doing. But though we may feel powerless, the Lord reminds us it is "in [our] power" to do good. As Paul testified, human weakness is an opportunity to know Christ's power at work in us (see 2 Cor. 12:9). The minutes in line at the bank, hours in the hospital recovery room, and years with a struggling child are not worthless, nor do they keep us from important work. Even there, God has prepared good works—such as prayer, generosity, encouragement, evangelism, and discipleship—for us to do (see Eph. 2:10). In our weariness and weakness, as we cry out to him in faith, he equips us by his Spirit and shows us how we can serve him in this moment. In the power of Christ and for the glory of Christ, we can do good while we wait.

Reflect: Identify the good works you are the most tempted to neglect in your current season of waiting. In what ways are you tempted to "withhold good" from people around you? When do you try to excuse yourself from doing good?

Reflect: Read Acts 16:25–34. Notice how Paul and Silas's imprisonment was the occasion for vital ministry. What were the men doing while they waited? How did they do good to their jailer? What did God accomplish through Paul and Silas?

Act: Use a moment of waiting to do good to someone today. While you are standing in line at the grocery store, text an encouraging Bible verse or a reminder of your care to a struggling church member. While you are stopped in traffic, pray for the salvation of your unbelieving neighbor.

DAY 22

Seek Wisdom

Whoever is slow to anger has great understanding, but he who has a hasty temper exalts folly. (Prov. 14:29)

ALTHOUGH HE HAD been anointed king when he was a boy, David waited many years to take the throne. During that time, he patiently endured mistreatment, hunger, danger, slander, and exile. Finally, after Saul's death, it seemed like the long wait was over, and he could begin to reign over Judah. But, even then, David did not act hastily. Instead, "David inquired of the LORD, 'Shall I go up into any of the cities of Judah?' And the LORD said to him, 'Go up.' David said, 'To which shall I go up?' And he said, 'To Hebron.' So David went up there" (2 Sam. 2:1–2). David knew that in order to rightly pursue a change in his circumstances, he needed wisdom from God.

While we are waiting on the Lord, one of our most important responsibilities is to get wisdom. Patience doesn't mean we never act; patience means we act carefully. And, for that, we need wisdom. We need wisdom to know when to speak and when to remain silent, when to pursue something new and when to be content with what we have, when to seek justice and when to overlook an offense. Even when we must act quickly, we need to proceed thoughtfully. As we practice patience, we receive the Bible's repeated exhortation to "get wisdom, and whatever you get, get insight" (Prov. 4:7).

Wisdom keeps us from foolish anger (as we see in today's verse) and from other kinds of rash responses. Experiencing unmet desires, unjust suffering, and unwanted circumstances, we often look for the quickest way out, even if it's through the door marked *Folly*. By contrast, the way of wisdom may not produce immediate results, but it will produce lasting ones. Wisdom enables us to be "peaceable, gentle, open to reason, full of mercy and good fruits, impartial and sincere" (James 3:17). It shields us, guards us, watches over us, delivers us, and lays out for us the path of life (see Prov. 2:7, 8, 12, 19). The wise life may not be the fast life or the flashy life, but it is ultimately the good life.

Thankfully, the source of true wisdom is readily available. The Bible is clear that wisdom is from the Lord (see Prov. 2:6), and so, like David, we must inquire of him. When we cry out to him in prayer, humbly acknowledging that we lack wisdom and asking him to provide (see James 1:5), he assures us that he will. He gives us Christ, who is the fount of all wisdom (see Col. 2:3). He gives us the indwelling Spirit, who trains our hearts to love what is good and hate what is evil. He gives us his Word, making it a lamp to our feet and a light to our path (see Ps. 119:105). He gives us an "abundance of counselors"—his people who help us by their wise guidance (Prov. 24:6). As we avail ourselves of his gracious means, God supplies all the wisdom we need.

Reflect: Patience doesn't mean we never take action; patience means we act wisely. In what area of your life do you need wisdom to know how to proceed?

Reflect: Read James 1:5–8. Ask God to give you wisdom.

Act: Identify a few wise people in your local church whom you can tell about your current situation. Ask them to pray with you, and invite them to counsel you about whether you should continue to wait or take action.

DAY 23

Keep Loving

Above all, keep loving one another earnestly, since
love covers a multitude of sins. (1 Peter 4:8)

"There was a man who had two sons" (Luke 15:11). So
begins Jesus's famous story about the loving father whose children treat him poorly. His youngest son demands a share of the
family property and squanders it in a "far country" (v. 13). His
oldest son falsely accuses him of being ungenerous. The father's
response is the parable's plot twist. We expect him to meet the
younger son with an angry catalogue of his offenses and the
older son with an exasperated litany of everything he has taken
for granted. Instead, the father speaks kindly to both wayward
children. He responds with compassion, offers hugs and kisses,
and affirms each son's place in the family (see vv. 20, 22–24, 31).
Rather than nursing bitterness during the long wait for his youngest son, the father obviously cultivates kindness, and, at the first
opportunity, he expresses his love.

While we wait patiently in our own relationships, today's
verse calls us to grow in love for the people around us. Writing
to the churches scattered throughout Asia, Peter gives instructions in light of the fact that "the end of all things is at hand"
(1 Peter 4:7). Time is short, he says. Jesus is coming. You won't
have to wait forever. Therefore, God's people have work to do.
We ought to walk with care in this world—being self-controlled,
sober-minded, and prayerful (see 1 Peter 4:7). We also ought to
love others.

Loving other people—especially other believers, but also our
enemies and persecutors (see Matt. 5:44)—is not an incidental
practice. Peter tells us it's the thing we should do "above all," we

69

should "keep" doing it, and we should do it "earnestly." Elsewhere, Paul declares that three things will last forever: "Faith, hope, and love . . . but the greatest of these is love" (1 Cor. 13:13). The end of all things is at hand, this world is passing away, and loving one another remains the unchanging priority of believers.

Peter roots this command in the real-world difficulties of relationships in a fallen world. His exhortation to "*keep* loving one another" seems to acknowledge the fact that, often, we want to give up. Like the sons in Jesus's parable, even the people closest to us sometimes treat us very badly. Years of frustration and hurt can accumulate in our relationships, and "loving one another" is the last thing we want to do. But, Peter says, it's precisely because of sin that we ought to seek the Spirit's help to grow in love. Cultivating love—affirming one another's value, welcoming and serving others, and taking God's glory more seriously than our own hurts (see 1 Peter 4:9–11)—enables us to overlook "a multitude of sins."

While you wait, keep loving.

Reflect: It's often easier to overlook the sins of someone whom we dearly love than those of a stranger or passing acquaintance. In what ways are patience and love connected in your own life?

Reflect: "Greet one another with a holy kiss" (Rom. 16:16). Five times the New Testament writers command Christians to express affection each time they see one another.[1] How would it change our interactions with other believers if we began every conversation with affirmation of our mutual love?

Act: Practice expressing love for others, especially in the church. Make it a habit to say, "It's so good to see you," to smile, or to give a hug or warm handshake. Allow your (situationally appropriate) demonstration of affection to remind you that each person is beloved of God and ought to be loved by you.

DAY 24

Hold On to Hope

*But if we hope for what we do not see, we wait
for it with patience. (Rom. 8:25)*

ONCE, ON A mountain hike in Connecticut, I encountered another family. The path was rocky and steep, the day was hot, and the family's young son was having difficulty keeping up. He sighed with every step, and tears sprang to his tired eyes. Coming alongside him, the father bent down to look the little boy in the face. He patted the bulging pocket of his backpack, and he spoke gently to his son: "Just keep thinking about that candy bar, Eli."

When the boy's endurance flagged, his wise father knew just how to encourage him: a concealed chocolate treat to savor at the mountain's peak. In today's verse, the Lord holds out for his own weary children a yet-to-be-revealed hope that enables us to persevere. Though we "groan inwardly" now, he calls us to meditate on our future glory "with eager longing" (Rom. 8:19, 23) so we will remain steadfast until the day of our complete redemption. While we wait, we must hold on to hope.

Paul's words in Romans 8 plainly acknowledge the difficulty of life in this world. The "sufferings of this present time" (v. 18) are real, and we groan under them. When we work for God's glory but see little fruit, when we cling to faith in Christ in the face of opposition or doubts, and when we persist in righteousness despite difficult circumstances, it's hard. But Paul reminds us that our groanings aren't merely *because of* our trials; our groanings are propelling us *toward* our future. Like labor pains (and the moans that accompany them), our current suffering is taking us to an immeasurably precious goal: our glorification (see vv. 21–23).

Far greater than a candy bar on a mountaintop, the future

"redemption of our bodies" (v. 23) is the hope that allows us to put one foot in front of the other today. Of course, our redemption was secured by Christ on the cross and applied to us at the moment of our new birth, but, in this life, it still remains partially hidden. Our spiritual transformation is both now and not yet: "Beloved, we are God's children now, and what we will be has not yet appeared; but we know that when he appears we shall be like him, because we shall see him as he is" (1 John 3:2).

And so, not only do we groan, but we also "wait eagerly" (Rom. 8:23). Like Zacchaeus, we abandon all dignity to shimmy up the nearest tree in order to fix our eyes on our Savior (see Luke 19:1–10). Like the psalmist, we nearly faint with longing to be in the near presence of the Lord (see Ps. 84:2). Like Paul and Silas, we sing the songs of heaven from the prison cells of earth (see Acts 16:25). One day, faith will be made sight and our hidden salvation will be fully revealed. Until then, we make it our hope, waiting for it with patience.

Reflect: John Calvin wrote that "hope . . . draws patience with it."[1] What is an event you've eagerly anticipated? How did having a promised future joy enable you to persevere in the present?

Reflect: Read Revelation 21:1–8. What are the new heavens and the new earth like? What gives you assurance that this heavenly vision will come to pass? How is the Lord's promise that the new Jerusalem is the inheritance of "the one who conquers" (v. 7) an encouragement to steadfastness?

Act: Keep thinking about the glory that awaits you.

DAY 25

Pray Persistently

And he told them a parable to the effect that they ought always to pray and not lose heart. (Luke 18:1)

YOU DON'T HAVE to spend long in a hospital waiting room before you realize there's not much to do. After you've flipped through the tattered copies of *People* or *Sports Illustrated* and glanced at the *Judge Judy* rerun on the TV, you are basically out of options. If you've thought to bring a book, you can read a few pages—provided you can concentrate. Otherwise, you might pull out your phone and scroll social media, but even that won't sustain your interest for more than a few minutes. At some point, if you have to sit there long enough, you'll probably come to the conclusion that there's nothing to do but wait.

Not every kind of waiting confines you to an uncomfortable vinyl chair in a windowless room, but all waiting can leave you with the same feeling of powerless futility. When waiting for your spouse to come to Christ, for a potential employer to notice your resume, or for your hostile neighbor to stop causing trouble, it often seems like there's not much you can do. And the longer the situation drags on, the fewer options you appear to have.

In Luke 18, Jesus told a parable about a widow who was also out of options. Alone in the world and without standing in her community, she had no obvious recourse when an "adversary" (v. 3) began mistreating her. Her only hope was to enlist the help of the judge in her city. Knowing this, she persisted in approaching him even when she didn't get immediate results. Finally, because of her "continual coming" (v. 5), the judge did what she asked.

Jesus told this story to encourage us to pray persistently. When we are weak and vulnerable—and we suspect that we can do nothing—we can pray. Our sovereign God directs all our circumstances. And so, like the widow with the judge, we ought to keep coming to God with our needs. We are powerless, but he is all-powerful. We lack wisdom, but he is all-wise. We can do nothing, but he can do all his holy will. Therefore, we have reason to pray "always" (Luke 18:1), "day and night" (Luke 18:7), "without ceasing" (1 Thess. 5:17), and "at all times" (Eph. 6:18). Unlike the judge, the Lord loves to hear his people's persistent prayers. Our constant coming doesn't bother him; he delights in it. In prayer, we "take no rest and give him no rest" because he welcomes it (Isa. 62:6–7).

Today's verse teaches us that patience is neither inaction nor capitulation; patience is humbly praying to the One who will act on our behalf. And when we pray for things agreeable to his will, he promises we will not have to wait long for an answer (see Luke 18:7–8). In contrast to the lazy and indifferent judge, the Lord always gives his children what is best at exactly the right time. Do not lose heart.

Reflect: Why is it easy to give up on prayer?

Reflect: Read Matthew 7:7–11. What three verbs does verse 7 use to describe prayer? What do those words teach us about how we ought to approach God? What is the Father's inclination toward us? How does this knowledge encourage you to pray boldly and persistently?

Act: Approach God in prayer today, and tomorrow, and the day after that. Remember that he is not a grudging public official but a gracious Father who loves to give his children what is best.

CULTIVATING PATIENCE IN SPECIFIC CIRCUMSTANCES

Patience is cultivated not in a vacuum but in the specific struggles of our lives on this earth. Over the next few days, we will consider how to wait well in a few common circumstances that often tempt us to impatience.

DAY 26

Patient in Deferred Hope

*The Lord is good to those who wait for him, to the soul
who seeks him. It is good that one should wait quietly
for the salvation of the Lord. (Lam. 3:25–26)*

A FEW YEARS AGO, my state's registry of motor vehicles
launched a campaign to encourage people to complete their reg-
istration and license renewals via the RMV website instead of vis-
iting a branch office. The tagline for the ads was "Skip the Line.
Go Online!"[1] Widely displayed on billboards, the catchy couplet
appealed to the famously fast-driving, horn-honking motorists of
my state. In Massachusetts, nobody wants to wait.

But it's not just Bay State residents who don't like delay, and
it's not just license plates we want. Most of us would prefer to have
all our desires met within the shortest period possible. Waiting
for the salvation of loved ones, the restoration of relationships,
or the fruit of our labors can feel like it drags on forever. Day after
day, the longed-for wedding or clean bill of health seems to slip
ever further into the future. "Hope deferred makes the heart sick,"
acknowledged Solomon in one of his proverbs (Prov. 13:12).
We'd all like to skip the line.

But while not denying that waiting is hard, today's verses
greet us with an unexpected counterpoint: waiting is good. Here,
Jeremiah hints at three ways waiting on the Lord is actually a
blessing.

First, as we wait, we experience God's goodness. "The Lord
is good to those who wait for him," Jeremiah declares. In our seasons of waiting, the Lord shows us tenderness and faithfulness we
couldn't experience in any other way. Had Jonah never waited for
three long days in the whale's belly, he wouldn't have known the

Lord as the one who hears us in distress, who delivers us from the pit, and who maintains his steadfast love even in the sea's depths (Jonah 2:1–9). Deferred hope may be our best opportunity to learn God's character.

Second, waiting weans us from the world and reorients us toward the Lord. When we don't immediately receive what we want, we have an opportunity to realize it might not be as important as we think. Cultivating a "soul who seeks [God]" and a heart that waits "quietly" allows us to consider the true priorities of our lives. After Hannah waited years for a child, she determined to give her son back to the Lord (see 1 Sam. 1:11). Waiting reminds us that the things we desire are simply instruments for the purposes of our God.

Finally, each wait trains us to wait for the fulfillment of our greatest desire, "the salvation of the LORD." In Psalm 27, surrounded by an army of evildoers, David simultaneously waited for two things: temporal deliverance and eternal deliverance. He allowed his earthly waiting to train him to wait patiently for the "one thing" he most desired: to be with God and to worship him forever (Ps. 27:4). Waiting on each of our lesser desires is practice for waiting well to the end.

It is good to wait.

Reflect: What good things have you experienced while waiting?

Reflect: Read 1 Samuel 1:1–2:11. Where did Hannah turn while she waited? What did Hannah's decision about Samuel demonstrate about her priorities? What truths about God's character did Hannah learn during her season of waiting?

Act: As you wait in line today—at the drive-through, on hold on the phone, at the doctor's office—praise God for his faithfulness. Sing a hymn, read a psalm, or simply thank God in prayer.

DAY 27

Patient in Affliction

So we do not lose heart. Though our outer self is wasting away, our inner self is being renewed day by day. For this light momentary affliction is preparing for us an eternal weight of glory beyond all comparison, as we look not to the things that are seen but to the things that are unseen. (2 Cor. 4:16–18)

PERHAPS NO BIBLICAL character is more famous for patience than Job. "You have heard of the steadfastness of Job," writes James (5:11), assuming that if his readers had even a basic knowledge of the Bible, they would know something about Job's patience. Most likely, they also knew something about Job's hardships: losing his property, his livelihood, his children, and his health (see Job 1:13–19; 2:7–8). In the story of Job, patience and trials are inextricably connected.

Afflictions come in many forms. In our lives, we suffer physically, financially, relationally, and spiritually in ways that mirror Job's own difficulties. Like Job, we don't always know the specific reason for our hardships, but today's verses give us hope that our afflictions are not pointless. Here, Paul points to four things God does as we remain steadfast under trials.

First, God renews us. It's no secret that hardships deplete, disorient, and discourage us. But if our afflictions are changing us, God is also changing us. He is renewing our inner selves: revealing himself to us in his Word, giving us his Spirit, and conforming us to the image of his Son. We may look bedraggled on the outside, but our inner selves are "being transformed . . . from one degree of glory to another" (2 Cor. 3:18).

Second, God prepares us. Our afflictions weigh heavily on us. They demand our time and our energy; they make us tired. But

Paul tells us that bearing their weight builds our spiritual muscles to receive the weight of glory. As our difficulties expose our sin and cast us on Christ, we prepare for eternity. With that in view, today's afflictions should seem "light [and] momentary"—the minor discomfort of daily exercise that readies us to win Olympic gold.

Third, God refocuses us. Hardship often grabs us by the cheeks and tries to point our attention solely at itself. "'What shall we eat?' or 'What shall we drink?' or 'What shall we wear?'" becomes our frantic litany as we stare at our circumstances (Matt. 6:31). But God uses trials to focus his afflicted people on something else: "The things that are unseen." As our bodies and our bank accounts fail, we are learning to place our hope in God alone.

Fourth, God strengthens us. When we "do not lose heart" today, we gain resources to remain steadfast tomorrow. As we practice patience today—trusting God and obeying his Word in the midst of affliction—the Lord equips us to withstand difficulty tomorrow. By the help of the Spirit, we "go from strength to strength, till each appears before God in Zion" (Ps. 84:7 NIV).

Reflect: In Psalm 119, David wrote, "It is good for me that I was afflicted" (v. 71). In what way can you testify to this truth in your own life?

Reflect: Read 2 Corinthians 11:24–33 and 12:7–10. List some of the afflictions that Paul experienced. How does it encourage you to know that the author of today's verses was familiar with extreme suffering?

Act: As you face pain and suffering today, cry out to the Lord. Ask him to remind you by his Word and Spirit that he loves you and is doing good things in your life—even in affliction.

DAY 28

Patient in Stagnant Seasons

*I am suffering, bound with chains as a criminal. But the word
of God is not bound! Therefore I endure everything for the
sake of the elect, that they also may obtain the salvation that
is in Christ Jesus with eternal glory. (2 Tim. 2:9–10)*

IN THE CARTOON version of a prison sentence, a pitiful fig-
ure in black-and-white stripes scratches a tally on the wall of his
cell. No sooner has the door clanged shut behind him than he
begins his count. As his beard grows and his shoulders slump,
the prisoner's tiny marks multiply around the room, each scratch
representing a day rendered meaningless except for the fact of its
passing.

Many of us feel like we are simply marking time too. It
may not be the bars of a cell that hold us captive; unreward-
ing employment or long days spent changing diapers can seem
equally limiting. If your town has few opportunities, your mar-
riage lacks sparkle, or your church's membership is dwindling,
it can feel like the walls are closing in. It's hard to remain patient
when you're stuck.

Today's verses come to us from an actual prison, and they
remind us that our stagnant seasons are not as limiting as they
may seem. Imprisoned for a second time in Rome, Paul wrote
frankly about his situation. He was suffering, chained, and
unjustly treated. Although he was both a gifted preacher and a
skilled tentmaker, the emperor's decree meant Paul was unable to
do either freely. Paul was bound.

But rather than fidgeting with his chains—or raging against
them—Paul affirmed his great hope: he may have been bound,
but "the word of God is not bound!" Paul's circumstances did not

prevent the Spirit from using the Scriptures to minister to Paul's heart. Later in the same letter, prisoner Paul makes his boldest declaration about the Bible's value, calling it "profitable for teaching, for reproof, for correction, and for training in righteousness" (3:16) and testifying to its usefulness for perfectly equipping us (v. 17). Like Paul, we can take courage that the Word of God is not bound by our stagnant circumstances. As we read it, meditate on it, and make it our delight, it will work freely in our hearts.

God's Word wasn't bound in Paul's life, and it wasn't bound in the lives of the people around him either. Though chained, he used every opportunity to declare the glory of Christ crucified. From another prison, he testified that "what has happened to me has really served to advance the gospel," allowing his guards and companions to hear the saving Word (Phil. 1:12–13). Like Paul, we can proclaim Christ to others no matter our situation. Our gospel witness in mundane moments may be the surprising instrument by which the elect obtain salvation "with eternal glory." Therefore, we endure.

Reflect: What opportunities do you have to savor God's Word? What opportunities do you have to point others to Christ?

Reflect: Read Romans 16:1–16. How does it encourage you to remember that the Lord uses ordinary, faithful Christians for great good in his kingdom?

Act: Author and missionary Elisabeth Elliot popularized an old poem whose refrain was "Do the next thing."[1] With these words, she reminded discouraged Christians that doing *something*—even the most mundane task—for God's glory is often the way of obedience. Lawnmowing and emails gain significance when we recognize them as God's calling in this moment. Today, when you feel frustrated about your situation, "do the next thing" with gospel hope.

DAY 29

Patient with the Weak

*And we urge you, brothers and sisters, admonish the idle, encourage the
fainthearted, help the weak, be patient with them all. (1 Thess. 5:14)*

THE CONCLUDING WORDS of Paul's first epistle to the Thessalonians contain a smattering of family rules. If the church is a
family—and it is!—these verses are an agenda for the family meeting, a family code of conduct posted on the refrigerator, family
goals calligraphed and framed over the kitchen table. Intended to
be read out to the whole assembly (see 1 Thess. 5:27), these imperatives identify behavior that is fitting for God's people in the local
church. They include instructions to honor elders, seek peace, do
good, pray, give thanks, and abstain from sin. And in the middle of
this list is an exhortation to patience: "Be patient with them all."

Scripture is unfailingly candid about life in "the household of
faith" (Gal. 6:10), and today's verse acknowledges that we share
the pews with a variety of difficult believers. We worship and work
alongside people who are undisciplined, who are fearful and doubting, and who keep falling into sin. These people require our time
and demand our energy. They blurt out awkward things in Bible
study, they're at the center of church drama, and they often make
us want to pull out our hair. There are frustrating people in God's
family, Paul acknowledges, and knowing how to relate to each person takes wisdom. But, ultimately, we need to bear with all of them.

Tomorrow we'll consider how to relate to people who deliberately sin against us, but today we'll see what God's Word says
about our conduct toward people who are simply careless, unreliable, or immature. The motivation for patience toward the weak
comes from Paul's term of address: "brothers and sisters." Just as
we don't get to choose the members of our biological famiies,[1]

we don't get to choose the members of our spiritual family either. And just as being part of a biological family obligates us to care for one another, being part of the church requires us to cultivate love for other believers.

This doesn't mean it's always easy to bear with our Christian brothers and sisters. For that, we need the help of another sibling—One who dwells in us by his Spirit and who is conforming us to his own image. Christ, our brother, is patient with all who come to him by faith. He is patient with us, and he looks with love at even the immature members of his church. "He is not ashamed to call them brothers and sisters" (Heb. 2:11) because he is perfecting each one. In Christ's family, we wait patiently, knowing that every member will one day be made like him.

Reflect: Tertullian famously imagined first-century Romans marveling at the early church, "See, how those Christians love one another!" Would the members of your community say this about your local church? Would they say it about you? Why or why not?

Reflect: Read 1 Corinthians 12:14–26. How is the good of all the members of the church interconnected? Paul affirms that "the parts of the body that seem to be weaker are indispensable" (v. 22). How would your conduct toward the weak change if you believed they were essential to the church family? Paul also writes, "On those parts of the body that we think less honorable we bestow the greater honor" (v. 23). How would your attitude toward immature Christians change if you made it a habit to honor them with your words and actions?

Act: Reach out to any members of your church whom you sometimes find frustrating. Ask them how they are doing, look for ways to encourage them, and tell them that you will be praying for them. Look forward to the day when they (and you!) will be like Christ.

Patient with People
Who Sin against You

Beloved, never avenge yourselves, but leave it to the wrath of God, for it is written, "Vengeance is mine, I will repay, says the Lord." (Rom. 12:19)

"HE HIT ME FIRST!" is a protest familiar to nearly every parent. When the dust settles around the bruises, young combatants scramble to point a finger anywhere but at their own hearts. In the retelling, the tussle on the living room floor wasn't a brawl but a perfectly reasonable judicial process. Whatever happened after the first punch was simply justice.

Today's verse speaks to everyone's instinct to rationalize impatient responses to being sinned against. When people defraud us, slander us, manipulate us, envy us, speak harshly to us, or begrudge us good, our first inclination is to react in anger. "He hit me first!" rises from our hearts as we seek the nearest opportunity to get back at our enemy and call it justified. But the Lord looks at our flushed cheeks and clenched fists and speaks a gentle word: "Beloved, never avenge yourselves."

Our revenge can take a variety of forms. In his sermon on long-suffering, Jonathan Edwards warned his hearers, "There are many ways in which men do that which is revengeful; not merely by bringing some immediate suffering on the one that may have injured them, but by anything, either in speech or behavior which [shows] a bitterness of spirit against him for what he has done."[1] Thinking or speaking resentfully of our enemies, failing to do good to them, or treating them harshly are all temptations we must resist.

To be clear, the Lord doesn't forbid careful steps to secure justice. The daughters of Zelophehad petitioned Israel's leaders for their inheritance, Peter and John argued their case in court, and Paul appealed to Caesar (see Num. 27:1–11; Acts 4:1–22; 25:1–12). Scripture affirms that we have a duty at times to confront sinners for their souls' good, and it even tells us how to do so (see Matt. 18:15–17). In these verses, though, the Lord forbids "repay[ing] . . . evil for evil" (Rom. 12:17)—making a sinful response to sinful behavior.

Rather than avenging ourselves, we must patiently wait for the Lord to do what he is going to do. Sometimes that means allowing civil or church authorities to act as God's instruments to bring a measure of justice in this life. Other times it means waiting for the final day of God's justice, when, "at the set time, [he] . . . will judge with equity" (Ps. 75:2). The sins of those who mistreat us *will* be avenged—either laid on the shoulders of the crucified Christ or counted against those sinners on the last day. But it's beyond us to know what God has chosen to do, and so we wait patiently, affirming with Abraham, "Shall not the Judge of all the earth do what is just?" (Gen. 18:25).

Reflect: "Revenge is sweet" is the misguided mantra of our age. When have you wrongly believed this?

Reflect: Read Proverbs 16:32. When we are sinned against, we often think it's an admission of weakness to overlook the offense. But this verse testifies that a patient person is actually mighty and powerful. In what way is this true? How would it change your response to being mistreated if you remembered this?

Act: When someone sins against you today, instead of focusing on your own injuries, remember the times you have sinned against the Lord. Thank him for his long-suffering toward you, ask him to continue to bear patiently with you, and look forward to the day when you will sin no more.

DAY 31

Patient Together

*I wait for the LORD, my soul waits, and in his word I hope. . . .
O Israel, hope in the LORD! For with the LORD there is steadfast
love, and with him is plentiful redemption. (Ps. 130:5, 7)*

ONCE, AT THE end of a workday, a potentially dangerous situation in my office meant I had to call the police. I was freshly graduated from college and living in an unfamiliar town. The thought of waiting alone in a dark building for the police to investigate was terrifying. Thankfully, my coworker heard about it on her way out. Coat in hand, she sat down next to me in the deserted hallway. "I'll wait with you," she said.

The situation turned out to be harmless, but my friend's faithful presence made a lasting impression on me. Few things are more comforting to those who wait than having someone to wait with. Simply by taking a seat for the duration, friends can calm our anxieties and redirect our frantic thoughts. With smiles on their faces or hands on our arms, they remind us that we are not alone. And as they speak words of truth, the slow-moving moments become bearable.

After seeking to cultivate patience over the past month, we'll see today that our experience with patience is not just for our own benefit. Having waited—and even while we continue to wait—we can sympathetically wait with others. In Psalm 130, one of the songs Israelites would sing together on their way to worship, the psalmist begins by retelling his own difficult situation. Mired in trouble and sin, he called out to the Lord for deliverance (see vv. 1–6). Nothing about his story sounds easy: he pleaded for mercy (see v. 2), he looked repeatedly for the Lord's help (see v. 6), and he waited and waited and waited (see vv. 5–6).

But in the midst of his long wait, he also experienced God's goodness. Psalm 130 shows he learned the horror of sin and the sweetness of God's long-suffering and forgiveness (see vv. 3–4). He turned to the Word of God and found a source of hope (see v. 5). He delighted in the Lord day by day and grew to love his appearing (see v. 6; cf. 2 Tim. 4:8).

This, in turn, prepared him to encourage others. In today's verses, the psalmist moves from recounting his own season of waiting to calling on the people of God to wait with hope. "O Israel," he says, "hope in the LORD!" Because he knew the difficulty of waiting, he could come alongside others who struggled to wait well. And because he had received God's grace while he waited, he could confidently testify to the truth of God's goodness so others might be encouraged (see vv. 7–8).

The same is true for us. Having known the Lord's mercy ourselves, we can strengthen others, sympathizing with them and testifying to the steadfast love of the Lord. We can take a seat next to them, reach out a hand, and gently say, "I'll wait with you."

Reflect: Why does waiting often feel lonely? Think of a time when you were helped by having a friend to wait with.

Reflect: Read Psalm 130. How did the psalmist's experience with waiting allow him to encourage the rest of God's people to wait well? What opportunities do you have to encourage fellow Christians in your church and community as they wait on the Lord?

Act: As you sing with your church this week, let the psalms' and hymns' truths about God's goodness and sovereignty give you courage. Sing heartily for God's glory—and encourage the people around you.

Conclusion

EVERY DAY, multiple times a day, we each answer the same question: What sounds good? We answer it when we peer into the refrigerator, searching for ingredients for tonight's dinner. We answer it when we make plans with a friend or a lunch meeting with a client. We answer it with every book we select at the library, every movie we queue in our watch list, and every song we add to our streaming service. We want a good paint color for the front door, a good school for our kids, a good church for our family. If we have an option, we rarely choose something that sounds bad. All of us are on a mission to increase the number of good things in our lives.

Of course, it's not always easy to determine what is good. Selecting a movie or paint color may be fairly simple, but the larger questions of what kind of people we ought to be and how we ought to live can leave us feeling uncertain. Thankfully, God's Word makes it abundantly clear that patience is good.

Over the past month, we have seen that God intends for us to grow in patience. Whether we are waiting on him to answer our prayers, persevering under afflictions, or bearing with other people, we don't have to scratch our heads about what would be good to do. Patience is always the right answer.

Best of all, our good God delights to cultivate patience in us. It is the fruit of his indwelling Spirit (see Gal. 5:22) and the mark of his perfecting grace (see James 1:4). We become patient people, not by gritting our teeth and tugging on our own bootstraps, but by casting ourselves on the Lord. And when we do, we will find that he is rich in mercy toward those who seek him.

Day by day, by the grace of God, we practice patience. And at the end of time, we will look back over our years of waiting and join with all of God's people to testify,

The LORD is good to those who wait for him,
    to the soul who seeks him.
It is good that one should wait quietly
    for the salvation of the LORD. (Lam. 3:25–26)

Beloved, the patient life is a very good life.

Notes

Day 1: Patience Is Waiting on the Lord

1. God, of course, exists outside time and is not bound by it. But he created time, placed his creation in time, and works in time to accomplish his purposes.

Day 2: Patience Is Steadfastness

1. John D. Legg, "John G. Paton," in *Five Pioneer Missionaries*, ed. S. M. Houghton (1965; repr., Carlisle, PA: Banner of Truth Trust, 1999), 303–45.

Day 6: God Commands Patience

1. For a helpful explanation of the use of God's law in the life of the believer, see the Westminster Confession of Faith, chapter 19.6.
2. John Murray, "Definitive Sanctification," in *Collected Writings of John Murray*, vol. 2, *Select Lectures in Systematic Theology* (1977; repr., Carlisle, PA: Banner of Truth Trust, 1996), 277–84.

Day 9: God Rewards Patience

1. For a helpful explanation of why God accepts our imperfect good works, see the Westminster Confession of Faith, chapter 16.6.

Day 11: Christ, Our Sympathetic Friend

1. C. S. Lewis, *Mere Christianity* (1952; repr., New York: Macmillan, 1977), 124.

Day 12: Christ, Our Power

1. Some of the sentences in this paragraph are adapted from my book *Contentment: Seeing God's Goodness*, 31-Day Devotionals for Life (Phillipsburg, NJ: P&R Publishing, 2018), 28.

Day 13: Christ's Glory, Our Hope

1. Jen Wilkin, *In His Image: 10 Ways God Calls Us to Reflect His Character* (Wheaton, IL: Crossway, 2018), 114.

Day 15: Afflictions Are Temporary
1. Melissa B. Kruger has reminded me of this on more than one occasion. I'm grateful for her wisdom.

Day 16: Human Souls Have Eternal Value
1. *Catechism for Young Children: Original Edition* (Lawrenceville, GA: Committee for Christian Education and Publications, 2020), question and answer 19.

Day 18: Every Moment of Your Life Has Value
1. Quoted by Desiring God (@desiringGod), Twitter, November 8, 2012, 11:56 a.m., https://twitter.com/desiringgod/status/26658 4993881550849?lang=en.

Day 21: Do Good
1. Janet Adamy, "Will a Twist on an Old Vow Deliver for Domino's Pizza?" *Wall Street Journal*, December 17, 2007, https://www.wsj .com/articles/SB119784843600332539.

Day 23: Keep Loving
1. Rom. 16:16; 1 Cor. 16:20; 2 Cor. 13:12; 1 Thess. 5:26; 1 Peter 5:14. A kiss was the typical expression of affection between first-century believers. While we may or may not kiss one another in our own local churches today, depending on our context, we affirm the principle of these commands with other morally chaste and culturally appropriate expressions such as a warm handshake or a hand on an arm.

Day 24: Hold On to Hope
1. John Calvin, *Calvin's Commentaries*, vol. 19, *Acts 14–28; Romans 1–16* (1974; repr., Grand Rapids: Baker Books, 1999), 310.

Day 26: Patient in Deferred Hope
1. Klark Jessen, "RMV Launches Campaign: Skip the Line, Go Online!" *MassDOT Blog*, October 1, 2015, https://blog.mass .gov/transportation/rmv/rmv-launches-campaign-skip-the-line -go-online/.

Day 28: Patient in Stagnant Seasons

1. Justin Taylor, "Do the Next Thing," *Between Two Worlds* (blog), Gospel Coalition, October 25, 2017, https://www.tgc.org/blogs/justin-taylor/do-the-next-thing/.

Day 29: Patient with the Weak

1. As the mother of two children by birth and two by adoption, I am daily grateful that God sometimes chooses to form families out of people with no biological relationship to one another. I use the term "biological family" simply as a contrast to "spiritual family," and I don't intend to discount the variety of family dynamics that exist in the world.

Day 30: Patient with People Who Sin against You

1. Jonathan Edwards, "Lecture IV: Charity Disposes Us Meekly to Bear the Injuries Received from Others," in *Charity and Its Fruits* (1852; repr., Carlisle, PA: Banner of Truth Trust, 2005), 71.

Suggested Resources for the Fight

Edwards, Jonathan. "Lecture IV: Charity Disposes Us Meekly to Bear the Injuries Received from Others." In *Charity and Its Fruits*, 66–95. 1852. Reprint, Carlisle, PA: Banner of Truth Trust, 2005. [Preaching on 1 Corinthians 13:4, "Love is patient," Edwards unflinchingly lays out the various ways that people can harm us, acknowledges our likely objections to loving our enemies, and exhorts us to nevertheless cultivate the fruit of long-suffering with the help of the Holy Spirit.]

Hill, Megan. *Contentment: Seeing God's Goodness*. 31-Day Devotionals for Life. Phillipsburg, NJ: P&R Publishing, 2018. [Often, we become impatient when we believe that God has not given us what is best. In this book, I unmask the sin of discontent and point to our God-given resources to overcome it.]

Houghton, S. M., ed. *Five Pioneer Missionaries*. 1965. Reprint, Carlisle, PA: Banner of Truth Trust, 1999. [If you want to learn about patience, read a missionary biography. This book tells the stories of five early modern missionaries who each persisted despite hardship for the cause of Christ and his church. As you learn their stories, you'll be encouraged to remain steadfast in your own.]

Ortlund, Dane. *Gentle and Lowly: The Heart of Christ for Sinners and Sufferers*. Wheaton, IL: Crossway, 2020. [Drawing especially from the work of Puritans like Thomas Goodwin and Richard Sibbes, this book explores the tender and patient way the Savior cares for his beloved people—even when we are weak or sinful. Savoring our Lord's love for us will kindle our desire to be patient with others.]

Wilkin, Jen. "God Most Patient." In *In His Image: 10 Ways God Calls Us to Reflect His Character*, 109–20. Wheaton, IL: Crossway, 2018. [God is patient, and this is the primary foundation for our own patience. In this brief chapter, Jen Wilkin helpfully explains what it means for God to be patient with us—and how we ought to imitate him.]

BIBLICAL COUNSELING COALITION

The Biblical Counseling Coalition (BCC) is passionate about enhancing and advancing biblical counseling globally. We accomplish this through broadcasting, connecting, and collaborating.

Broadcasting promotes gospel-centered biblical counseling ministries and resources to bring hope and healing to hurting people around the world. We promote biblical counseling in a number of ways: through our *15:14* podcast, website (biblicalcounselingcoalition.org), partner ministry, conference attendance, and personal relationships.

Connecting biblical counselors and biblical counseling ministries is a central component of the BCC. The BCC was founded by leaders in the biblical counseling movement who saw the need for and the power behind building a strong global network of biblical counselors. We introduce individuals and ministries to one another to establish gospel-centered relationships.

Collaboration is the natural outgrowth of our connecting efforts. We truly believe that biblical counselors and ministries can accomplish more by working together. The BCC Confessional Statement, which is a clear and comprehensive definition of biblical counseling, was created through the cooperative effort of over thirty leading biblical counselors. The BCC has also published a three-part series of multi-contributor works that bring theological wisdom and practical expertise to pastors, church leaders, counseling practitioners, and students. Each year we are able to facilitate the production of numerous resources, including books, articles, videos, audio resources, and a host of other helps for biblical counselors. Working together allows us to provide robust resources and develop best practices in biblical counseling so that we can hone the ministry of soul care in the church.

To learn more about the BCC, visit biblicalcounselingcoalition.org.

Also by Megan Hill in the 31-Day Devotionals for Life Series

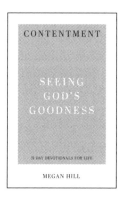

The world pressures us to fulfill our desires—but God tells us to master them through contentment. This practical daily devotional helps us to cultivate thankfulness in situations that fuel discontent.

"Megan Hill comes to the rescue with a practical daily devotional full of how-to's and why-to's [and], more importantly . . . the 'who' of a daily relationship with Jesus Christ."
—**David Murray**, Professor of Old Testament and Practical Theology, Puritan Reformed Theological Seminary

"Helps those who are longing to shed the weight of discontent by pointing them to the soul-satisfying contentment found in Jesus Christ."
—**Christina Fox**, Author, *A Heart Set Free*

"With clear, practical, biblical reflection, Hill leads us to the greener pastures of Christian contentment."
—**Jen Pollock Michel**, Author, *Teach Us to Want*

Did you find this book helpful?
Consider leaving a review online.
The author appreciates your feedback!

Or write to P&R at editorial@prpbooks.com
with your comments. We'd love to hear from you.